Table of Contents

Editor's Note

"Where we love is home—home that our feet may leave, but not our hearts."

—Oliver Wendell Holmes, Sr.

Donald A. Gardner has been designing homes for more than 35 years, and it shows. His flair for artistic detail and passion for architectural design is evident in every one of his firm's quality residential designs. From quaint cozy cottages to expansive elegant estates, each plan is crafted with the same attention to detail. Whether big or small, we see at a glance that Mr. Gardner designs homes for today's families: comfortable country and traditional exteriors are combined with beautiful interiors designed to meet the needs of our busy lives. But there is more to his designs than four walls; each plan is conceived with the realization that it will become your "home," your sanctuary, your retreat from the world. With this clear commitment to the needs of the heart and hearth, it's not surprising his designs are proven winners with homeowners all over North America. His many successes include the following:

❖ Best Selling Designer awards from Home Planners for 1997 & 1998

❖ Overall Best Selling Designer awards from *Builder* magazine for 1996 & 1998

❖ Best Selling Plan awards from Home Planners for 1997 & 1998

❖ Best Selling Plan awards from *Builder* magazine for 1992, 1993, 1994, 1996 & 1997

❖ 1996 National Certificate of Merit from the American Institute of Architects for
  The Hampton at Highland Creek

Captured within these pages are many of Donald Gardner's most popular designs: adorable country homes with delightful dormers and wide covered porches perfect for soft summer evenings spent watching the stars; traditional treasures with stately exteriors and open interiors, offering a sense of gracious hospitality as well as stylish comfort. Alongside these family favorites, we are delighted to showcase many of Mr. Gardner's newest designs. Look for the cedar shakes, wood siding and natural materials that distinguish the rustic character of his Craftsman-style homes. If you have in mind a design specifically suited to a sloping site, notice his exciting line of hillside homes. And for those with an eye toward more palatial accommodations, we know you will find the perfect plan among his gracious estates—luxurious homes more than three thousand square feet. Frank Lloyd Wright once said, "Buildings should bring people joy." Whatever dream house you have in mind, there is a "home" within these pages that will fulfill that ideal. Enjoy!

Heart Collection

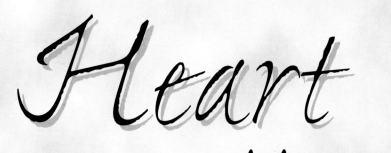

A gallery of picture-perfect homes

THE *Arbordale*

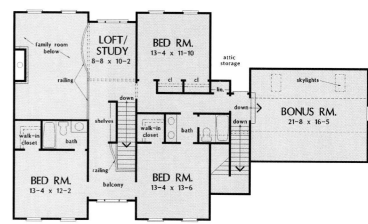

- LOFT/ STUDY 8-8 x 10-2
- family room below
- railing
- BED RM. 13-4 x 11-10
- attic storage
- cl cl lin.
- down
- shelves
- walk-in closet
- bath
- walk-in closet
- bath
- down
- down
- skylights
- BONUS RM. 21-8 x 16-5
- BED RM. 13-4 x 12-2
- railing
- balcony
- BED RM. 13-4 x 13-6

WIDTH 81'-10"
DEPTH 51'-8"

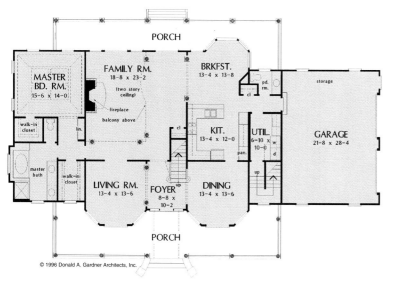

- PORCH
- MASTER BD. RM. 15-6 x 14-0
- FAMILY RM. 18-8 x 23-2
- (two story ceiling)
- fireplace
- balcony above
- BRKFST. 13-4 x 13-8
- pd. rm.
- cl
- storage
- walk-in closet
- lin.
- cl
- KIT. 13-4 x 12-0
- UTIL. 6-10 x 10-0
- w d
- pan.
- GARAGE 21-8 x 28-4
- master bath
- walk-in closet
- LIVING RM. 13-4 x 13-6
- FOYER 8-8 x 10-2
- DINING 13-4 x 13-6
- up
- up
- PORCH

© 1996 Donald A. Gardner Architects, Inc.

This home, as shown in the photographs, may differ from the actual blueprints. For more detailed information, please check the floor plans carefully.

Rear View

Photos by Riley & Riley Photography, Inc.

This beautiful farmhouse with prominent twin gables and bays adds just the right amount of country style to modern family life. The master suite is quietly tucked away downstairs with no rooms directly above, and the cook of the family will love the spacious U-shaped kitchen. The bonus room is easily accessible from the back stairs or second floor, where three large bedrooms share two full baths. A curved balcony borders a versatile loft/study, which overlooks the stunning two-story great room. *For similar plans, please see Design 7656 on pages 96-97 and Design 7769 on pages 94-95.*

DESIGN 7650

MAIN LEVEL: 2,086 square feet
UPPER LEVEL: 1,077 square feet
TOTAL: 3,163 square feet
BONUS ROOM: 403 square feet

Left: The open loft/study overlooks a stunning family room, which features double French doors to the rear porch.

Right: This private corner suite is enhanced by a fresh array of delicate florals, sunshine-yellow walls and convenient deck access.

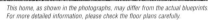

THE *Irwin*

*T*his attractive four-bedroom house offers a touch of country with its covered front porch. The foyer, flanked by the dining room and the bedroom/study, leads to the spacious great room. The dining room and breakfast room have cathedral ceilings with arched windows filling the house with natural light. The master bedroom boasts a cathedral ceiling and bath with whirlpool tub, shower and double-bowl vanity. Two family bedrooms reside upstairs with a full bath. Please specify basement or crawlspace foundation when ordering.

Right: A beautiful tiled fireplace adds warmth and a sloped ceiling adds volume to the great room, made bright by plenty of windows.

Photos by Riley & Riley Photography, Inc.

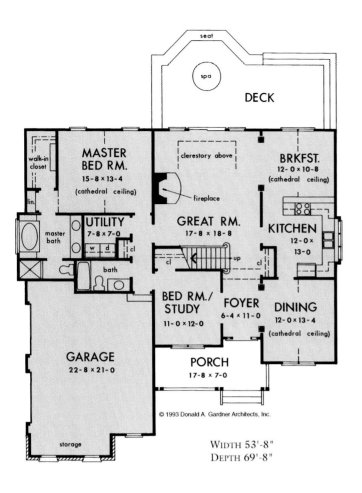

seat

spa

DECK

MASTER
BED RM.
15-8 × 13-4
(cathedral ceiling)

walk-in
closet

lin.

master
bath

bath

UTILITY
7-8 × 7-0

w d

cl

clerestory above

fireplace

GREAT RM.
17-8 × 18-8

cl

up

cl

BRKFST.
12-0 × 10-8
(cathedral ceiling)

KITCHEN
12-0 ×
13-0

BED RM./
STUDY
11-0 × 12-0

FOYER
6-4 × 11-0

DINING
12-0 × 13-4
(cathedral ceiling)

GARAGE
22-8 × 21-0

PORCH
17-8 × 7-0

© 1993 Donald A. Gardner Architects, Inc.

storage

WIDTH 53'-8"
DEPTH 69'-8"

Above: A dramatic, honey-toned cathedral ceiling enhances the gracious main suite.

Just like cookies 'n' cream, this delicious kitchen will be a family favorite.

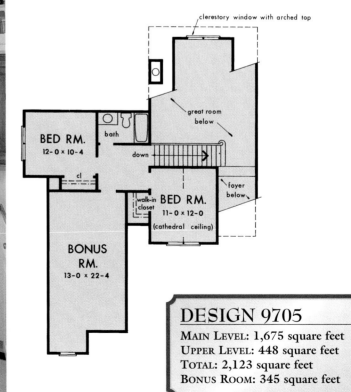

clerestory window with arched top

great room
below

BED RM.
12-0 × 10-4

bath

down

cl

walk-in
closet

foyer
below

BED RM.
11-0 × 12-0
(cathedral ceiling)

BONUS
RM.
13-0 × 22-4

DESIGN 9705

MAIN LEVEL: 1,675 square feet
UPPER LEVEL: 448 square feet
TOTAL: 2,123 square feet
BONUS ROOM: 345 square feet

Photos by Riley & Riley Photography, Inc.

THE *Altamont*

Right: Rich, wood cabinetry and burgundy-red counter-tops enhance this efficient kitchen, which opens to the sunny breakfast area and screened porch.

Left: A fresh mix of sparkling-white porcelain, lemon-fresh walls and forest-green tile creates a cheery atmosphere in the luxuriously proportioned main bath.

A neighborly porch as friendly as a handshake wraps around this charming country home, warmly greeting family and friends alike. Inside, cathedral ceilings promote a feeling of spaciousness. To the left of the foyer, the great room is enhanced with a fireplace and built-in bookshelves. A uniquely shaped formal dining room separates the kitchen and breakfast area. Outdoor pursuits, rain or shine, will be enjoyed from the screened porch. The master suite is located at the rear of the plan for privacy and features a walk-in closet and a luxurious bath. Two additional bedrooms, one with a walk-in closet, share a skylit bath. A second-floor bonus room is available to develop later as a study, home office or play area. Please specify basement or crawlspace foundation when ordering. *For similar plans, please see Design 9781 on page 55 and Design 9748 on pages 56-57.*

A wall of floor-to-ceiling windows brightens the octagon-shaped dining room, enriched by a warm blend of colors and textures.

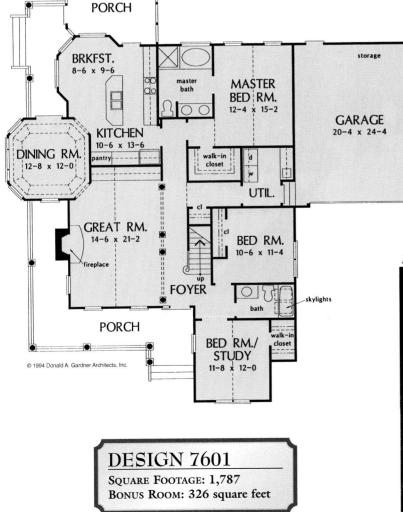

SCREEN PORCH

BRKFST.
8-6 x 9-6

master bath

MASTER BED RM.
12-4 x 15-2

storage

GARAGE
20-4 x 24-4

KITCHEN
10-6 x 13-6

pantry

DINING RM.
12-8 x 12-0

walk-in closet

d
w

UTIL.

cl

GREAT RM.
14-6 x 21-2

fireplace

cl

BED RM.
10-6 x 11-4

up

FOYER

bath

skylights

PORCH

BED RM./ STUDY
11-8 x 12-0

walk-in closet

© 1994 Donald A. Gardner Architects, Inc.

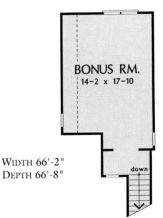

BONUS RM.
14-2 x 17-10

WIDTH 66'-2"
DEPTH 66'-8"

down

Rear View

DESIGN 7601

SQUARE FOOTAGE: 1,787
BONUS ROOM: 326 square feet

THE *Ingraham*

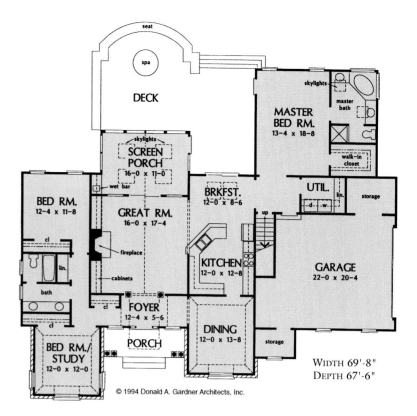

A two-story foyer with a Palladian window above sets the tone for this sunlit home. Columns mark the passage from the foyer to the great room, where a centered fireplace and built-in cabinets are found. A screened porch with four skylights above and a wet bar provides a pleasant place to start the day or wind down after work. The kitchen is flanked by the formal dining room and the breakfast room with sliding glass doors to the large, rear deck. Hidden quietly in the rear, the master suite includes a bath with dual vanities and skylights. Two family bedrooms (one an optional study) share a bath with twin sinks. Please specify basement or crawlspace foundation when ordering.

DESIGN 9734
SQUARE FOOTAGE: 1,977
BONUS ROOM: 430 square feet

© 1994 Donald A. Gardner Architects, Inc.

WIDTH 69'-8"
DEPTH 67'-6"

Photos by Riley & Riley Photography, Inc.

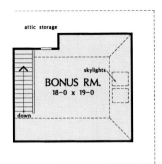

Rear View

Top right: Special features such as an elegant tray ceiling and a circle-top window allow you to entertain in style in the formal dining room.

Above: Enhanced by the rich patina of period-style furniture, the spacious main suite offers a comfortable retreat for the weary homeowner.

Left: The main bath's whirlpool tub is bathed in natural light from corner windows and an overhead skylight.

This home, as shown in the photographs, may differ from the actual blueprints. For more detailed information, please check the floor plans carefully.

THE *Hampton*

DESIGN 7742
SQUARE FOOTAGE: 1,879
BONUS ROOM: 360 square feet

Rear View

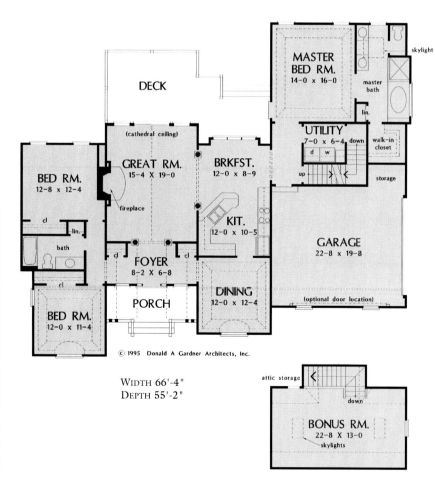

DECK

(cathedral ceiling)

MASTER BED RM.
14-0 x 16-0

skylight

master bath

lin.

UTILITY
7-0 x 6-4

down

walk-in closet

d   w

up

storage

BED RM.
12-8 x 12-4

GREAT RM.
15-4 X 19-0

BRKFST.
12-0 x 8-9

fireplace

KIT.
12-0 x 10-5

cl

lin.

bath

cl

FOYER
8-2 X 6-8

cl

GARAGE
22-8 x 19-8

cl

DINING
12-0 x 12-4

BED RM.
12-0 x 11-4

PORCH

(optional door location)

© 1995   Donald A Gardner Architects, Inc.

WIDTH 66'-4"
DEPTH 55'-2"

attic storage

down

BONUS RM.
22-8 X 13-0

skylights

ormers cast light and interest into the foyer for a grand first impression that sets the tone in a home full of today's amenities. The great room, articulated by columns, features a cathedral ceiling and is conveniently located adjacent to the breakfast room and kitchen. Tray ceilings and picture windows with circle tops accent the front bedroom and dining room. A secluded main suite, highlighted by a tray ceiling in the bedroom, includes a bath with skylight, garden tub, separate shower, double-bowl vanity and a spacious walk-in closet. *For similar plans, please see Design 9778 on pages 30-31 and Design 9726 on page 29.*

Above: Beautiful wood floors and cabinetry pair well with crisp white countertops in this sunny kitchen and breakfast area.

Top right: Unpretentious style defines the elegant great room, with its grand cathedral ceiling, classic columns and built-in cabinetry.

Right: Formal but definitely not stuffy, this golden-hued dining room gains distinction with a tray ceiling, chair-rail accent and a striking floor-to-ceiling circle-top window.

Photos by Riley & Riley Photography, Inc.

This home, as shown in the photographs, may differ from the actual blueprints. For more detailed information, please check the floor plans carefully.

THE *Stratford*

*T*his country home has more than just elegance, style and a host of amenities, it has heart. A cathedral ceiling highlights the great room, while a clerestory window and sliding glass doors really let in the light. Broad windows in the breakfast bay splash the L-shaped kitchen with natural light. The private main suite, with a tray ceiling and walk-in closet, boasts luxurious amenities: skylit bath, whirlpool tub, separate shower and dual vanities. Two additional bedrooms share a full bath. The front bedroom features a walk-in closet and could double as a study. *For similar plans, please see Design 9783 on pages 50-51 and Design 9782 on page 103.*

DESIGN 9779
SQUARE FOOTAGE: 1,632

WIDTH 62'-4"
DEPTH 55'-2"

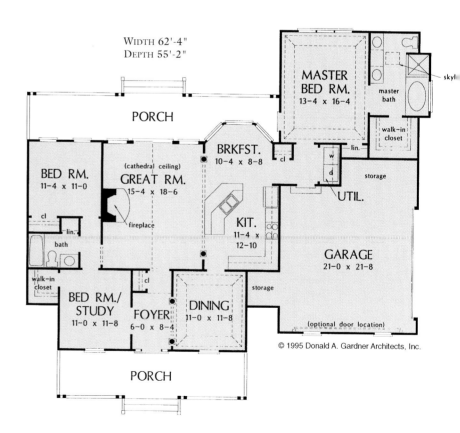

© 1995 Donald A. Gardner Architects, Inc.

Rear View

Left: An arch-top, clerestory window above a wall of glass enhances the great room, flooding this open area with natural light.

Above: Reverse view of the great room.

Right: Classic columns and an attractive tray ceiling accent the rose-hued dining room—a luxurious space for elegant occasions.

Dorm-estic Bliss

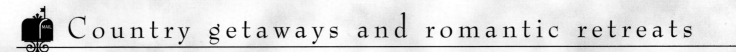 Country getaways and romantic retreats

$\mathcal{T}$his economical, rustic three-bedroom plan sports a relaxing country image with both front and back covered porches. The openness of the expansive great room to kitchen/dining areas and loft/study areas is reinforced with a shared cathedral ceiling for impressive space. The first level allows for two bedrooms, a full bath and a utility area. The main suite on the second level has a walk-in closet and a bath with whirlpool tub, shower and double-bowl vanity. Please specify basement or crawlspace foundation when ordering.

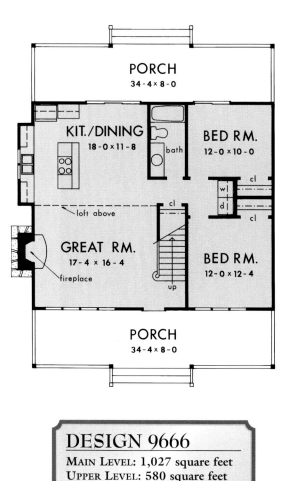

PORCH
34-4 × 8-0

KIT./DINING
18-0 × 11-8

bath

BED RM.
12-0 × 10-0

wl
d

cl

cl

cl

loft above

GREAT RM.
17-4 × 16-4

fireplace

up

BED RM.
12-0 × 12-4

PORCH
34-4 × 8-0

© 1992 Donald A. Gardner Architects, Inc.

LOFT/ STUDY
11-4 × 13-8

master bath

walk-in closet

STO.
3-4 × 6-4

railing

down

great room below

MASTER BED RM.
12-0 × 14-0

WIDTH 37'-4"
DEPTH 44'-8"

DESIGN 9666
MAIN LEVEL: 1,027 square feet
UPPER LEVEL: 580 square feet
TOTAL: 1,607 square feet

THE *Laurel*

© 1992 Donald A. Gardner Architects, Inc.

B. NATHAN.

THE *Seymour*

DESIGN 9697

MAIN LEVEL: 1,039 square feet
UPPER LEVEL: 583 square feet
TOTAL: 1,622 square feet

BED RM.
12-6 × 13-8

walk-in closet

bath

closet

railing

down

BED RM.
12-0 × 15-8

great room below

WIDTH 37'-9"
DEPTH 44'-8"

PORCH
34-6 × 8-0

KIT./
DINING
10-10 × 17-8

walk-in closet

w   d

MASTER
BED RM.
12-0 × 17-0

bedroom above

sto.

GREAT RM.
17-4 × 17-2

fireplace

up

cl

master bath

PORCH
34-6 × 8-0

© 1992 Donald A. Gardner Architects, Inc.

Charming and compact, this delightful two-story cabin is perfect for the small family or empty-nester. Designed with casual living in mind, the two-story great room is completely open to the dining area and the spacious island kitchen. The main suite is on the first floor for privacy and convenience. It features a roomy bath and a walk-in closet. Upstairs, two comfortable bedrooms—one has a dormer window, the other has a balcony overlooking the great room—share a full hall bath.

© 1998 Donald A. Gardner, Inc.

B. NATHAN

THE *Schuyler*

Twin clerestory dormers help create this home's classic country look, flooding the foyer, dining room and great room with natural light.

_T_he country charm of a front porch, gables and dormers combine with an open interior and split-bedroom design to give this home sensational appeal inside and out. The foyer, dining room, kitchen, breakfast nook and great room flow easily for an open, comfortable feel. A dramatic cathedral ceiling amplifies the great room and kitchen, while the breakfast area is enhanced by a beautiful box-bay window. The main suite is secluded at the back of the home and features deck access, two walk-in closets and a private bath. Two more bedrooms share a hall bath on the opposite side of the home.

DESIGN 7771
SQUARE FOOTAGE: 1,559

WIDTH 54'-4"
DEPTH 52'-0"

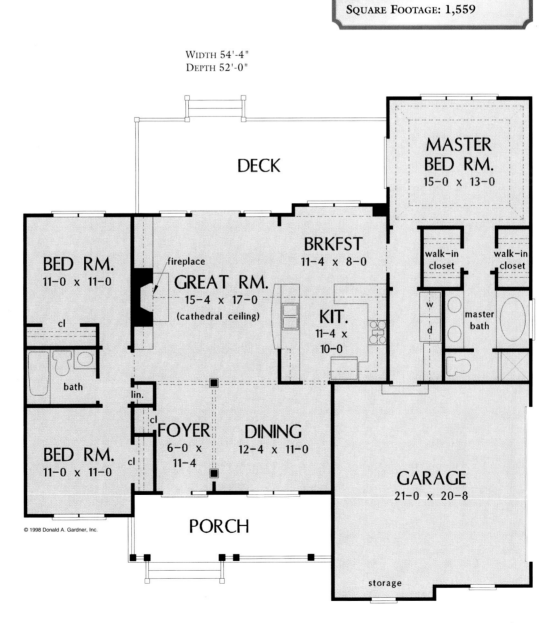

DECK

MASTER BED RM.
15-0 x 13-0

BED RM.
11-0 x 11-0

fireplace

GREAT RM.
15-4 x 17-0
(cathedral ceiling)

BRKFST
11-4 x 8-0

walk-in closet

walk-in closet

w
d

master bath

cl

bath

KIT.
11-4 x 10-0

lin.

cl

FOYER
6-0 x 11-4

DINING
12-4 x 11-0

cl

BED RM.
11-0 x 11-0

GARAGE
21-0 x 20-8

© 1998 Donald A. Gardner, Inc.

PORCH

storage

© 1994 Donald A. Gardner Architects, Inc.

THE *Aiken*

DESIGN 9753
SQUARE FOOTAGE: 1,346

REAR VIEW

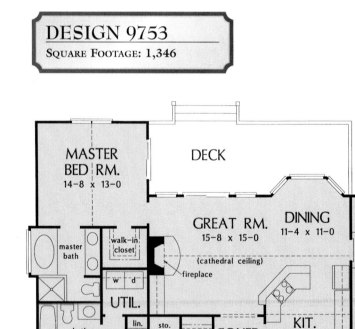

MASTER BED RM.
14-8 x 13-0

DECK

master bath

walk-in closet

GREAT RM.
15-8 x 15-0

DINING
11-4 x 11-0

(cathedral ceiling)

fireplace

w   d

UTIL.

bath

lin.

sto.

cl

FOYER
6-8 x 5-8

KIT.
11-4 x 12-4

GARAGE
21-0 x 21-0

cl

BED RM.
10-0 x 10-4

cl

BED RM.
10-0 x 10-4

PORCH

© 1994 Donald A. Gardner Architects, Inc.

WIDTH 65'-0"
DEPTH 44'-2"

A great room that stretches into the dining room makes this design perfect for entertaining. A fireplace and built-ins, as well as a cathedral ceiling, further enhance the possibilities. A rear deck allows for great outdoor livability. It can be reached from the main bedroom and the great room. The ample kitchen features lots of counter and cabinet space as well as an angled cooktop. Three bedrooms include a main suite with sloped ceiling, private bath and walk-in closet.

An inviting front porch, dormers, gables and windows topped by half-rounds give this home curb appeal, while inside, an open floor plan with split-bedroom design and a spacious bonus room steal the show. Two dormers add light and volume to the foyer, while a cathedral ceiling enlarges the open great room. Accent columns define the foyer, great room, kitchen and breakfast area. Both the dining room and the front bedroom/study have tray ceilings that show off stunning picture windows with half-rounds. The private main suite with a tray ceiling accesses the rear deck through sliding glass doors, and the bath includes a garden tub, separate shower and two skylights over a double-bowl vanity.

DESIGN 7719

SQUARE FOOTAGE: 1,699
BONUS ROOM: 336 square feet

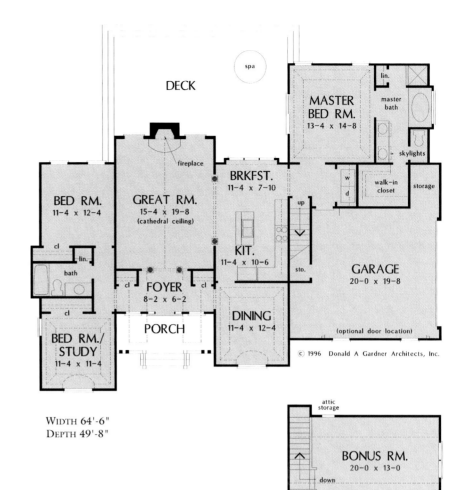

DECK

spa

MASTER BED RM.
13-4 x 14-8

lin.

master bath

skylights

BED RM.
11-4 x 12-4

GREAT RM.
15-4 x 19-8
(cathedral ceiling)

fireplace

BRKFST.
11-4 x 7-10

up

w
d

walk-in closet

storage

cl

lin.

bath

KIT.
11-4 x 10-6

sto.

GARAGE
20-0 x 19-8

cl

FOYER
8-2 x 6-2

cl

cl

DINING
11-4 x 12-4

(optional door location)

BED RM./ STUDY
11-4 x 11-4

PORCH

© 1996   Donald A Gardner Architects, Inc.

WIDTH 64'-6"
DEPTH 49'-8"

attic storage

BONUS RM.
20-0 x 13-0

down

attic storage

THE *Fairmont*

B. NATHAN

*S*tylish rooms and comfortable arrangements make this country home unique and inviting. The foyer opens from a quaint covered porch and leads to the expansive great room, which boasts a cathedral ceiling, an extended-hearth fireplace and access to the rear deck. The kitchen serves the formal dining room as well as the bayed breakfast nook, which offers windows that really bring in the outdoors. A secluded main suite nestles to the rear of the plan and features a U-shaped walk-in closet, a garden tub and twin vanities. Two nearby bedrooms—or make one a study—share a full bath and a gallery hall that leads back to the foyer.

DECK

MASTER BED RM.
14-8 x 13-4
(cathedral ceiling)

BRKFST.
11-0 x 9-5

fireplace

master bath

walk-in closet

(cathedral ceiling)

GREAT RM.
16-0 x 19-0

KIT.
11-4 x 10-7

GARAGE
21-0 x 23-4

w | d

UTIL.

bath

cl

balcony above

up

DINING
11-0 x 12-4

© 1995 Donald A. Gardner Architects, Inc.

lin.

cl

cl

FOYER
7-4 x 5-8

BED RM.
12-0 x 11-0

cl

BED RM./
STUDY
11-0 x 12-0
(cathedral ceiling)

PORCH

WIDTH 65'-4"
DEPTH 55'-4"

DESIGN 9794
SQUARE FOOTAGE: 1,633
BONUS ROOM: 595 square feet

great room below

(unfinished)
BONUS
14-8 x 17-0

(unfinished)
BONUS
11-0 x 12-4

down

railing

balcony (optional)

attic storage

MAIL

THE *Cleveland*

© 1995 Donald A. Gardner Architects, Inc.

B. NATHAN

© 1993 Donald A. Gardner Architects, Inc.

THE *Baldwin*

This charming country home utilizes multi-pane windows, columns, dormers and a covered porch to offer a welcoming front exterior. Inside, the great room with a dramatic cathedral ceiling commands attention; the kitchen and breakfast room are just beyond a set of columns. The tiered-ceilinged dining room presents a delightfully formal atmosphere for dinner parties or family gatherings. A tray ceiling in the main bedroom contributes to its pleasant atmosphere, as do the large walk-in closet and the gracious main bath with a garden tub and a separate shower. The secondary bedrooms are located at the opposite end of the house for privacy. Please specify basement or crawlspace foundation when ordering. *For similar plans, please see Design 7742 on pages 16-17 and Design 9778 on pages 30-31.*

© 1993 Donald A. Gardner Architects, Inc.

WIDTH 59'-8"
DEPTH 50'-8"

DESIGN 9726
SQUARE FOOTAGE: 1,498

© 1995 Donald A. Gardner Architects, Inc.

THE *Stockton*

A contemporary blend of town and country fuse past and present on this delightful design. A winsome facade features elements such as a covered porch supported by twin sets of pilasters, while an attractive entry leads to an open interior space.

REAR VIEW

DECK

spa

MASTER BED RM.
13-4 x 14-8

master bath

lin.

skylights

fireplace

GREAT RM.
15-4 x 19-8

(cathedral ceiling)

BRKFST.
11-4 x 8-0

w
d

walk-in closet

storage

BED RM.
11-4 x 12-4

cl

lin.

bath

cl

down

KIT.
11-4 x 10-4

GARAGE
20-0 x 19-8

cl

FOYER
8-2 x 6-2

cl

storage

cl

BED RM./ STUDY
11-4 x 11-4

PORCH

DINING
11-4 x 12-4

(optional door location)

© 1995 Donald A. Gardner Architects, Inc.

WIDTH 61'-0"
DEPTH 53'-8"

DESIGN 9778

SQUARE FOOTAGE: 1,655

Covered front porch dormers and arched windows welcome you to this modified version of one of our most popular country home plans. Interior columns dramatically open the foyer and the kitchen to the spacious great room. The drama is heightened by the great room's cathedral ceiling and fireplace. The kitchen, with its food preparation island, easily serves the breakfast room and the formal dining room. The main suite has a tray ceiling and access to the rear deck. Added luxuries include a walk-in closet and a skylit bath with a double vanity, a garden tub and a separate shower. Two generous bedrooms share the second bath. Please specify basement or crawlspace foundation when ordering. *For similar plans, please see Design 7742 on pages 16-17 and Design 9726 on page 29.*

© 1994 Donald A. Gardner Architects, Inc.

B. NATHAN

THE *Culver*

Special details enhance the charming exterior of this
country home. Shutters, muntins and a sunburst
accent dress up the front bedroom's eye-catching
picture window, capped by double gables.

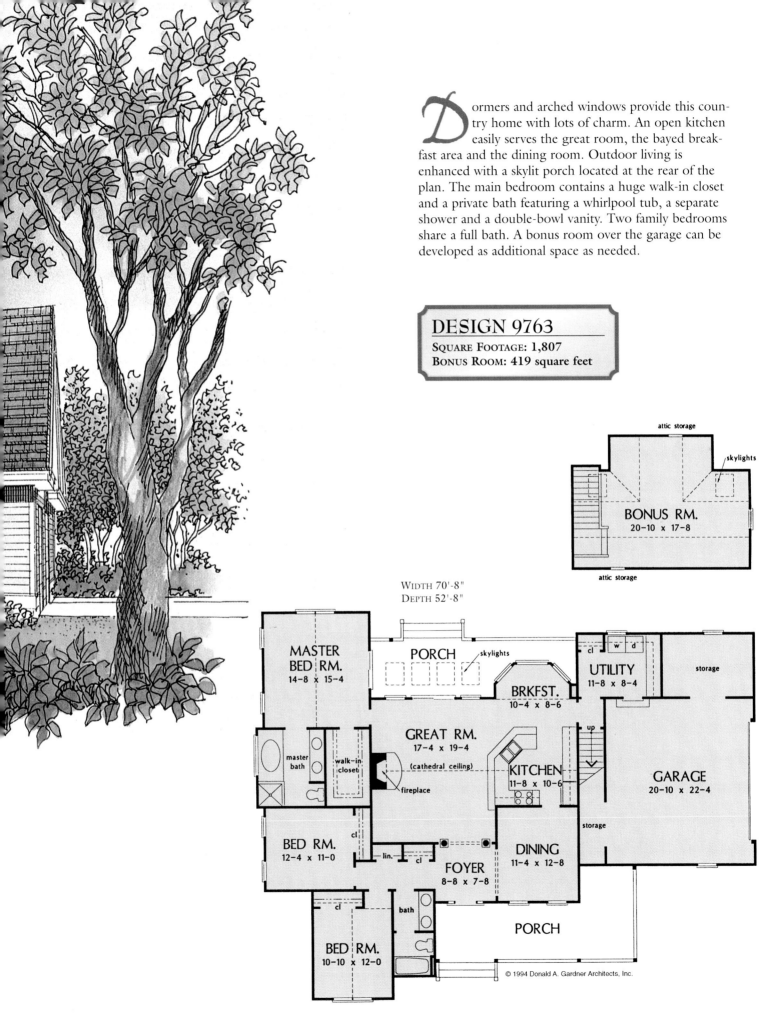

ormers and arched windows provide this country home with lots of charm. An open kitchen easily serves the great room, the bayed breakfast area and the dining room. Outdoor living is enhanced with a skylit porch located at the rear of the plan. The main bedroom contains a huge walk-in closet and a private bath featuring a whirlpool tub, a separate shower and a double-bowl vanity. Two family bedrooms share a full bath. A bonus room over the garage can be developed as additional space as needed.

DESIGN 9763
SQUARE FOOTAGE: 1,807
BONUS ROOM: 419 square feet

attic storage

skylights

BONUS RM.
20-10 x 17-8

attic storage

WIDTH 70'-8"
DEPTH 52'-8"

MASTER BED RM.
14-8 x 15-4

PORCH

skylights

BRKFST.
10-4 x 8-6

UTILITY
11-8 x 8-4

cl   w   d

storage

GREAT RM.
17-4 x 19-4

(cathedral ceiling)

fireplace

master bath

walk-in closet

KITCHEN
11-8 x 10-6

up

GARAGE
20-10 x 22-4

BED RM.
12-4 x 11-0

cl

lin.

cl

FOYER
8-8 x 7-8

DINING
11-4 x 12-8

storage

cl

bath

BED RM.
10-10 x 12-0

PORCH

© 1994 Donald A. Gardner Architects, Inc.

© 1994 Donald A. Gardner Architects, Inc.

B. NATHAN

THE *New Hope*

This modern farmhouse design enjoys a roomy covered porch, a perfect spot to place planters or colorful flower baskets. Imagine wood pillars adorned with flowering jasmine or wisteria—through open doors and windows, fragrant breezes will intoxicate your senses.

REAR VIEW

his quaint four-bedroom home with front and rear porches reinforces its beauty with arched windows and dormers. The pillared dining room opens on your right, while a study that could double as a guest room is available on your left. Straight ahead lies the massive great room with its cathedral ceiling, enchanting fireplace and access to the private rear porch and the deck with a spa and seat. Within steps of the dining room is the efficient kitchen and the sunny breakfast nook. The main suite enjoys a cathedral ceiling, rear deck access and a private bath with a skylit whirlpool tub, a walk-in closet and a double vanity. Two additional bedrooms are located at the opposite end of the house and share a full bath with dual vanities.

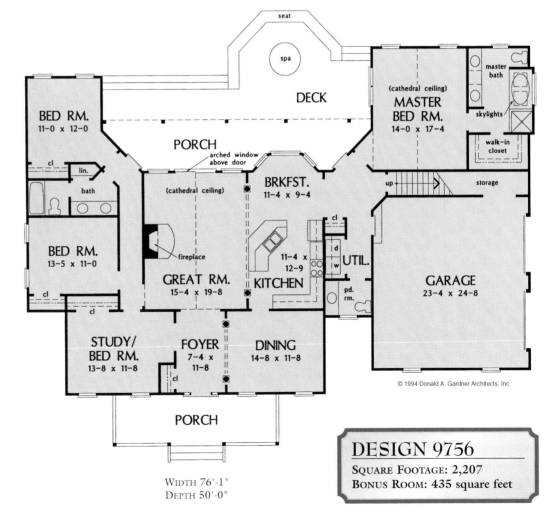

BONUS RM.
14-4 x 24-8

WIDTH 76'-1"
DEPTH 50'-0"

© 1994 Donald A. Gardner Architects, Inc.

DESIGN 9756
SQUARE FOOTAGE: 2,207
BONUS ROOM: 435 square feet

*Q*uaint and cozy on the outside with porches front and back, this three-bedroom country home surprises with an open floor plan featuring a large great room with a cathedral ceiling. Nine-foot ceilings add volume throughout the home. A central kitchen with an angled counter opens to the breakfast and great rooms for easy entertaining. The privately located main bedroom has a cathedral ceiling and access to the deck. Operable skylights over the tub accent the luxurious bath. Two secondary bedrooms share a full hall bath. A bonus room makes expanding easy. Please specify basement or crawlspace foundation when ordering.

REAR VIEW

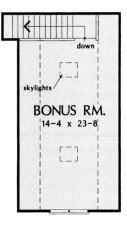

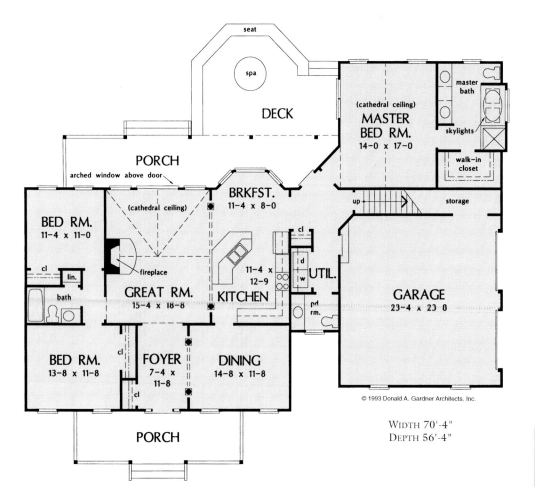

seat

spa

DECK

PORCH

arched window above door

(cathedral ceiling)

BRKFST.
11-4 x 8-0

(cathedral ceiling)

MASTER BED RM.
14-0 x 17-0

master bath

skylights

walk-in closet

up

storage

BED RM.
11-4 x 11-0

cl

lin.

bath

fireplace

11-4 x 12-9

GREAT RM.
15-4 x 18-8

KITCHEN

cl

d

w

UTIL.

pd rm.

GARAGE
23-4 x 23-0

BED RM.
13-8 x 11-8

cl

FOYER
7-4 x 11-8

cl

DINING
14-8 x 11-8

© 1993 Donald A. Gardner Architects, Inc.

PORCH

WIDTH 70'-4"
DEPTH 56'-4"

skylights

down

BONUS RM.
14-4 x 23-8

DESIGN 9749

SQUARE FOOTAGE: 1,864
BONUS ROOM: 420 square feet

© 1993 Donald A. Gardner Architects, Inc.

B. NATHAN.

THE *Pennyhill*

With easy living in mind, a covered porch provides the perfect spot to sit and watch the world go by. Attractive architectural details include wooden rails and columns on the porch, and Colonial-style muntins and shutters on the windows.

© 1994 Donald A. Gardner Architects, Inc.

THE *Halifax*

Horizontal siding, multi-pane windows and a wooden balustrade lend a prairies 'n' plains flavor to this traditional home. A paneled door with sidelights opens to flexible interior space.

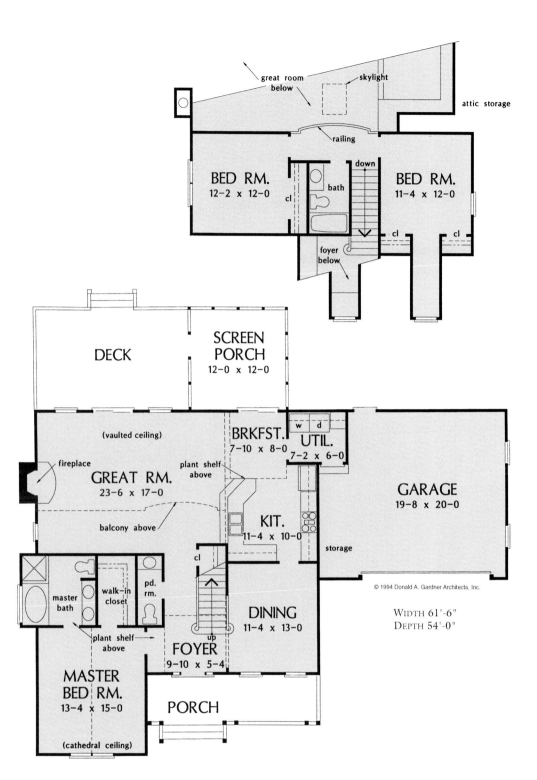

great room
below

skylight

attic storage

railing

BED RM.
12-2 x 12-0

cl

bath

down

BED RM.
11-4 x 12-0

cl

cl

foyer
below

DECK

SCREEN
PORCH
12-0 x 12-0

(vaulted ceiling)

BRKFST.
7-10 x 8-0

UTIL.
7-2 x 6-0

w   d

fireplace

GREAT RM.
23-6 x 17-0

plant shelf
above

GARAGE
19-8 x 20-0

KIT.
11-4 x 10-0

balcony above

storage

cl

master
bath

walk-in
closet

pd.
rm.

up

DINING
11-4 x 13-0

plant shelf
above

FOYER
9-10 x 5-4

© 1994 Donald A. Gardner Architects, Inc.

WIDTH 61'-6"
DEPTH 54'-0"

MASTER
BED RM.
13-4 x 15-0

PORCH

(cathedral ceiling)

DESIGN 9747
MAIN LEVEL: 1,335 square feet
UPPER LEVEL: 488 square feet
TOTAL: 1,823 square feet

*E*legant dormers and arch-topped windows offer a charming facade for this traditional design, with plenty of fabulous amenities to be found within. Lead guests leisurely through the foyer and central hall to a magnificent great room with vaulted ceiling and skylight, centered fireplace, decorative plant shelf and access to the rear deck. Attached to the nearby kitchen, a breakfast nook opens to a screened porch, perfect for informal alfesco dining. The well-appointed kitchen also serves the adjacent dining room on more formal occasions. A secluded first-floor main suite introduces high elegance with a cathedral ceiling and a Palladian-style window. A spacious walk-in closet, a whirlpool tub and a separate shower complete the comforts of this suite. Upstairs, a balcony hall connects two additional bedrooms, which share a full bath.

© 1998 Donald A. Gardner, Inc.

THE *Courtney*

Who ever said garages had to be boring? The comfortable exterior of this home is significantly enhanced by twin garage doors featuring multiple panels, overhead transoms and keystone accents.

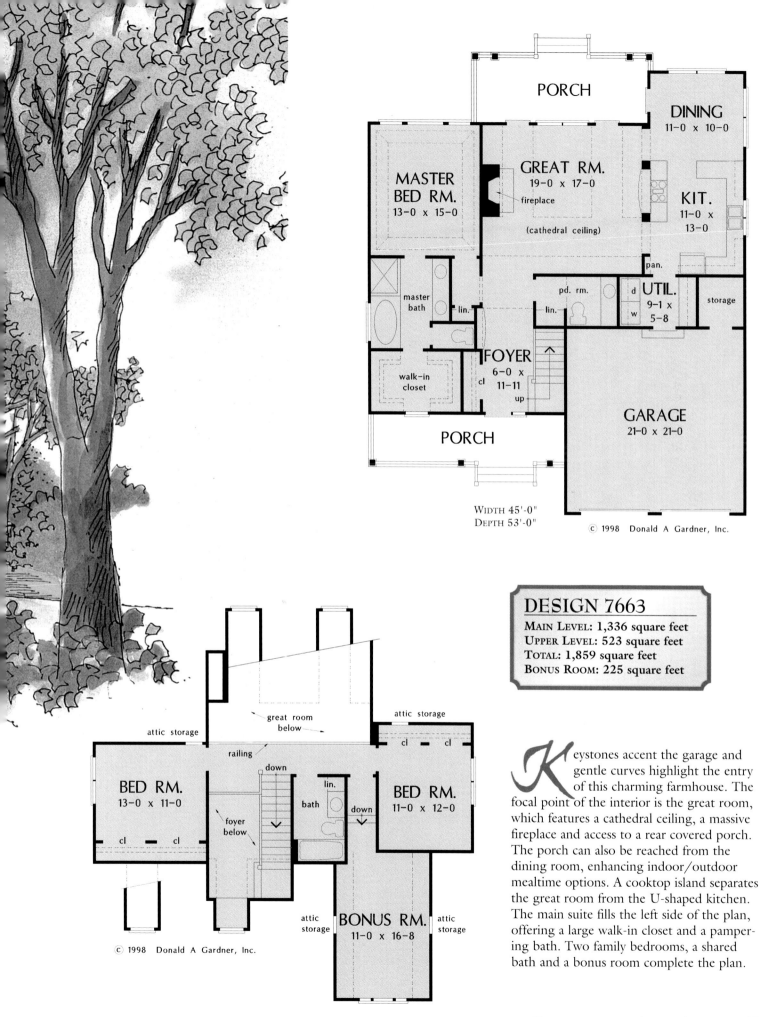

PORCH

DINING
11-0 x 10-0

MASTER
BED RM.
13-0 x 15-0

GREAT RM.
19-0 x 17-0

fireplace

KIT.
11-0 x
13-0

(cathedral ceiling)

pan.

master
bath

lin.

pd. rm.

lin.

d   UTIL.
9-1 x
w   5-8

storage

walk-in
closet

FOYER
6-0 x
11-11

cl

up

GARAGE
21-0 x 21-0

PORCH

WIDTH 45'-0"
DEPTH 53'-0"

© 1998 Donald A Gardner, Inc.

attic storage

great room
below

attic storage

railing

cl   cl

BED RM.
13-0 x 11-0

down

lin.

BED RM.
11-0 x 12-0

foyer
below

bath

down

cl   cl

attic
storage

BONUS RM.
11-0 x 16-8

attic
storage

© 1998 Donald A Gardner, Inc.

DESIGN 7663

MAIN LEVEL: 1,336 square feet
UPPER LEVEL: 523 square feet
TOTAL: 1,859 square feet
BONUS ROOM: 225 square feet

Keystones accent the garage and gentle curves highlight the entry of this charming farmhouse. The focal point of the interior is the great room, which features a cathedral ceiling, a massive fireplace and access to a rear covered porch. The porch can also be reached from the dining room, enhancing indoor/outdoor mealtime options. A cooktop island separates the great room from the U-shaped kitchen. The main suite fills the left side of the plan, offering a large walk-in closet and a pampering bath. Two family bedrooms, a shared bath and a bonus room complete the plan.

Country getaways and romantic retreats **41**

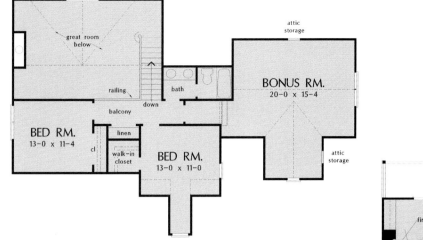

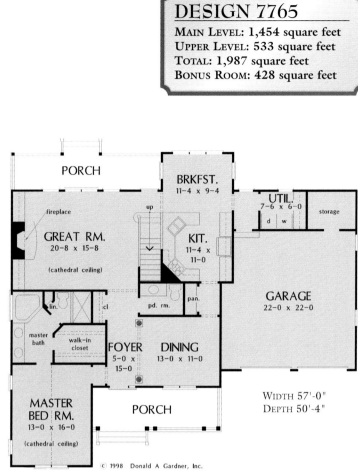

DESIGN 7765

MAIN LEVEL: 1,454 square feet
UPPER LEVEL: 533 square feet
TOTAL: 1,987 square feet
BONUS ROOM: 428 square feet

Arched windows, gables and dormers combine for maximum curb appeal outside, while inside, an innovative floor plan makes this home remarkably family friendly. Elegant columns divide the home's foyer from its formal dining room, which is separated from the kitchen by a sizable pantry. The great room features a cathedral ceiling, a fireplace with flanking built-ins and a wall of windows overlooking the back porch. The main suite enjoys privacy on the first floor as well as a cathedral ceiling, private bath and walk-in closet. Two more bedrooms upstairs share a hall bath, large linen closet and access to the bonus room.

THE *Coventry*

© 1998 Donald A. Gardner, Inc.

THE *Thornberry*

Amulti-pane bay window, decorative dormers and a covered porch dress up this one-story cottage. The entrance foyer leads to an impressive great room with cathedral ceiling and fireplace. The U-shaped kitchen, adjacent to the dining room, provides an ideal layout for food preparation. A large deck offers shelter while admitting cheery sunlight through skylights. A luxurious main bedroom, located to the rear of the house, takes advantage of the deck area and is assured privacy from two other bedrooms at the front of the house. These family bedrooms share a full bath.

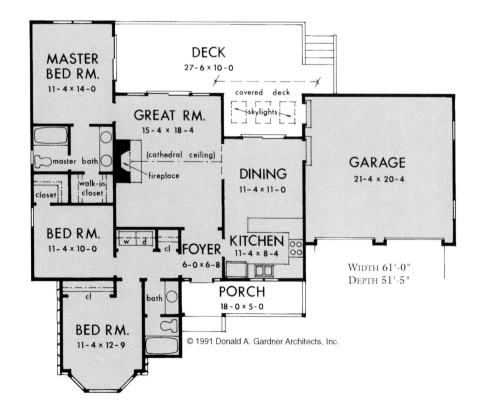

MASTER BED RM.
11-4 x 14-0

DECK
27-6 x 10-0

covered deck

skylights

GREAT RM.
15-4 x 18-4

(cathedral ceiling)

fireplace

master bath

walk-in closet

closet

DINING
11-4 x 11-0

GARAGE
21-4 x 20-4

BED RM.
11-4 x 10-0

w d

cl

FOYER
6-0 x 6-8

KITCHEN
11-4 x 8-4

cl

bath

BED RM.
11-4 x 12-9

PORCH
18-0 x 5-0

WIDTH 61'-0"
DEPTH 51'-5"

DESIGN 9620

SQUARE FOOTAGE: 1,310

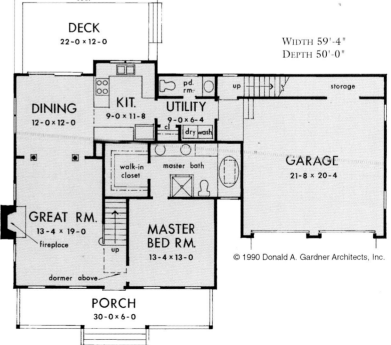

THE *Langford*

This compact, two-story, cozy country cottage is perfect for the economically conscious family. Its entrance foyer is highlighted by a clerestory dormer above for natural light. The main suite is conveniently located on the first level for privacy and accessibility. Its attached bath boasts a whirlpool tub with skylight above, a separate shower and a double-bowl vanity. Second-level bedrooms share a full bath and there's a wealth of storage on this level. An added advantage to this house is the bonus room above the garage. Please specify basement or crawl-space foundation when ordering.

DESIGN 9626

MAIN LEVEL: 1,057 square feet
UPPER LEVEL: 500 square feet
TOTAL: 1,557 square feet
BONUS ROOM: 342 square feet

down

BONUS RM.
14-4 × 23-8

attic storage

bath

BED RM.
13-4 × 10-8

down

BED RM.
13-4 × 10-8

cl   cl   cl   cl

seat

DECK
22-0 × 12-0

WIDTH 59'-4"
DEPTH 50'-0"

DINING
12-0 × 12-0

KIT.
9-0 × 11-8

pd. rm.

UTILITY
9-0 × 6-4

up

storage

cl

dry wash

walk-in closet

master bath

GARAGE
21-8 × 20-4

GREAT RM.
13-4 × 19-0

fireplace

up

MASTER BED RM.
13-4 × 13-0

© 1990 Donald A. Gardner Architects, Inc.

dormer above

PORCH
30-0 × 6-0

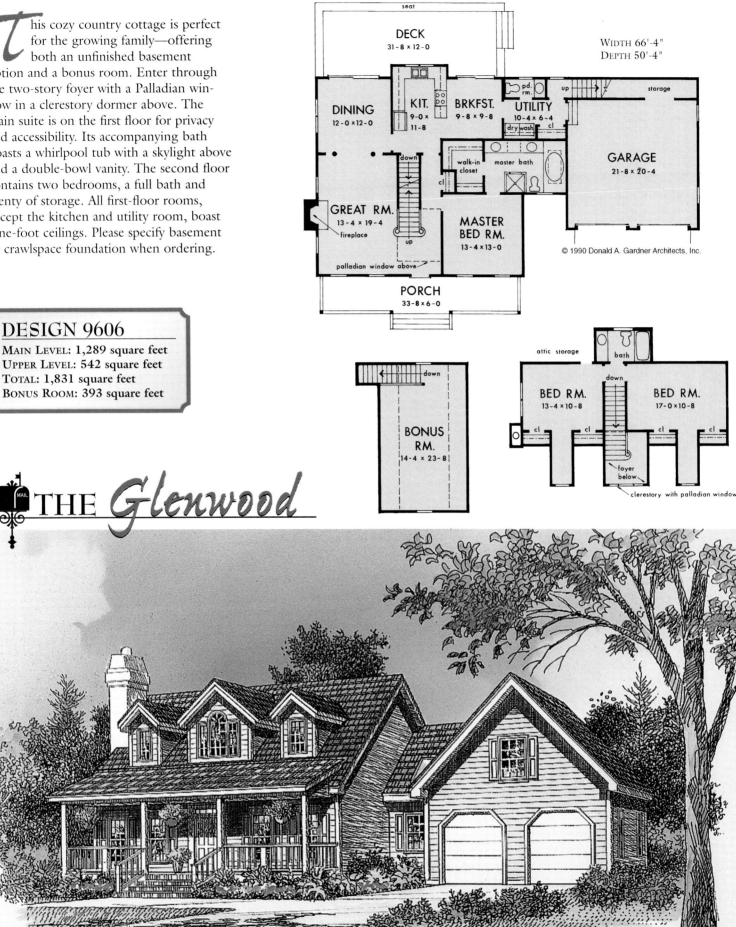

*T*his cozy country cottage is perfect for the growing family—offering both an unfinished basement option and a bonus room. Enter through the two-story foyer with a Palladian window in a clerestory dormer above. The main suite is on the first floor for privacy and accessibility. Its accompanying bath boasts a whirlpool tub with a skylight above and a double-bowl vanity. The second floor contains two bedrooms, a full bath and plenty of storage. All first-floor rooms, except the kitchen and utility room, boast nine-foot ceilings. Please specify basement or crawlspace foundation when ordering.

DECK
31-8 x 12-0

WIDTH 66'-4"
DEPTH 50'-4"

DINING
12-0 x 12-0

KIT.
9-0 x 11-8

BRKFST.
9-8 x 9-8

UTILITY
10-4 x 6-4

pd. rm.

up

storage

GREAT RM.
13-4 x 19-4

fireplace

walk-in closet

master bath

GARAGE
21-8 x 20-4

MASTER BED RM.
13-4 x 13-0

© 1990 Donald A. Gardner Architects, Inc.

palladian window above

PORCH
33-8 x 6-0

DESIGN 9606

MAIN LEVEL: 1,289 square feet
UPPER LEVEL: 542 square feet
TOTAL: 1,831 square feet
BONUS ROOM: 393 square feet

attic storage

bath

BED RM.
13-4 x 10-8

down

BED RM.
17-0 x 10-8

BONUS RM.
14-4 x 23-8

foyer below

clerestory with palladian window

THE *Glenwood*

© 1990 Donald A. Gardner Architects, Inc.

B. NATHAN

A trio of dormers with arch-topped windows and a country front porch adorn the facade of this gracious, three-bedroom home. Columns and a tray ceiling grant distinction and definition to the formal dining room, while the great room is enriched by a cathedral ceiling with two rear clerestory dormers, a fireplace and built-in bookshelves. The home's split-bedroom design provides plenty of privacy for the main suite, which features a tray ceiling, walk-in closet and deluxe bath. Two secondary bedrooms, one with back-porch access, share a hall bath with a linen closet.

DESIGN 7775
SQUARE FOOTAGE: 1,733
BONUS ROOM: 372 square feet

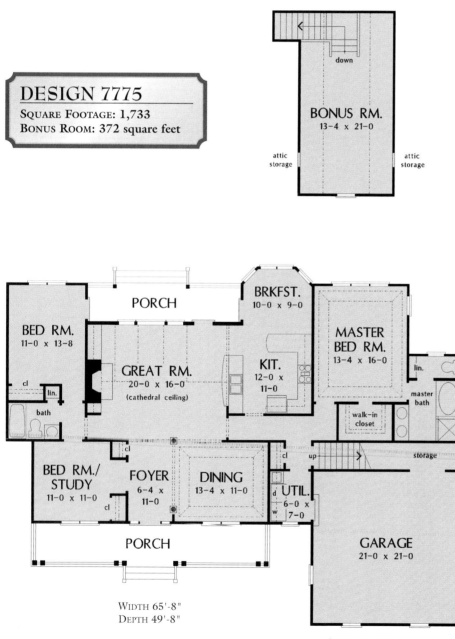

down

BONUS RM.
13-4 x 21-0

attic storage

attic storage

PORCH

BRKFST.
10-0 x 9-0

BED RM.
11-0 x 13-8

MASTER BED RM.
13-4 x 16-0

cl

lin.

lin.

GREAT RM.
20-0 x 16-0
(cathedral ceiling)

KIT.
12-0 x 11-0

master bath

bath

walk-in closet

cl

cl

up

storage

BED RM./ STUDY
11-0 x 11-0

FOYER
6-4 x 11-0

DINING
13-4 x 11-0

UTIL.
6-0 x 7-0

d

w

cl

PORCH

GARAGE
21-0 x 21-0

WIDTH 65'-8"
DEPTH 49'-8"

© 1998 Donald A Gardner, Inc.

© 1998 Donald A. Gardner, Inc.

B.NATHAN

THE *Riverbirch*

Without question, nothing captures the spirit of country living quite like a covered porch. There is a relaxed feeling about it, whether this design is intended for a rural retreat or a suburban street.

THE Redding

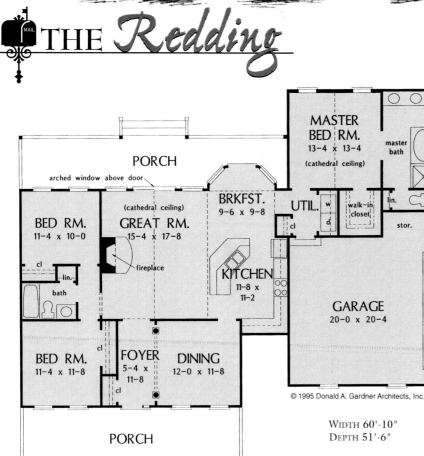

PORCH

arched window above door

BED RM.
11-4 x 10-0

GREAT RM.
15-4 x 17-8

(cathedral ceiling)

fireplace

cl
lin.
bath

BED RM.
11-4 x 11-8

cl

FOYER
5-4 x
11-8

cl

DINING
12-0 x 11-8

PORCH

BRKFST.
9-6 x 9-8

KITCHEN
11-8 x
11-2

MASTER
BED RM.
13-4 x 13-4

(cathedral ceiling)

UTIL.

w
d

master
bath

walk-in
closet

lin.

stor.

cl

GARAGE
20-0 x 20-4

© 1995 Donald A. Gardner Architects, Inc.

WIDTH 60'-10"
DEPTH 51'-6"

DESIGN 9780
SQUARE FOOTAGE: 1,561

Combining the finest country details with the most modern livability, this one-story home makes modest budgets really stretch. The welcoming front porch encourages you to stop and enjoy the summer breezes. The entry foyer leads to a formal dining room defined by columns. Beyond is the large great room with a cathedral ceiling and a fireplace. The kitchen and the breakfast room open to the living area and include porch access. The main suite is tucked away in its own private space. It is conveniently separated from the family bedrooms, which share a full bath. The two-car garage contains extra storage space.

REAR VIEW

THE *Henderson*

This lovely country home features ample closet space in the main bedroom and a bonus room. The main suite also has a tray ceiling and a private bath with a garden tub and a picture window. An open island kitchen and a great room with a cathedral ceiling split the main bedroom from two additional bedrooms. The formal dining room is dressed up with a tray ceiling, while outside, full front and back porches expand the living area.

WIDTH 62'-4"
DEPTH 57'-4"

skylight

MASTER BED RM.
13-4 x 16-4

master bath

lin.

walk-in closet

w
d

storage

PORCH

BRKFST.
11-4 x 8-8

GREAT RM.
15-4 x 18-6
(cathedral ceiling)

BED RM.
11-4 x 11-0

cl

fireplace

lin.

KIT.
11-4 x 12-10

up

bath

walk-in closet

BED RM./ STUDY
11-0 x 11-8

FOYER
6-0 x 8-4

cl

DINING
11-0 x 11-8

GARAGE
21-0 x 21-8

storage

PORCH

© 1996 Donald A Gardner Architects, Inc.

DESIGN 7711
SQUARE FOOTAGE: 1,685
BONUS ROOM: 331 square feet

down

BONUS RM.
12-0 x 21-8

attic storage

skylights

B. NATHAN

© 1996 Donald A. Gardner Architects, Inc.

REAR VIEW

© 1995 Donald A. Gardner Architects, Inc.

B. NATHAN.

THE *Georgetown*

In keeping with the rest of this home's design, the garage boasts special exterior details. A distinctive gable caps multi-paned, shuttered windows—an attractive round-top window floods an upstairs bonus room with natural light.

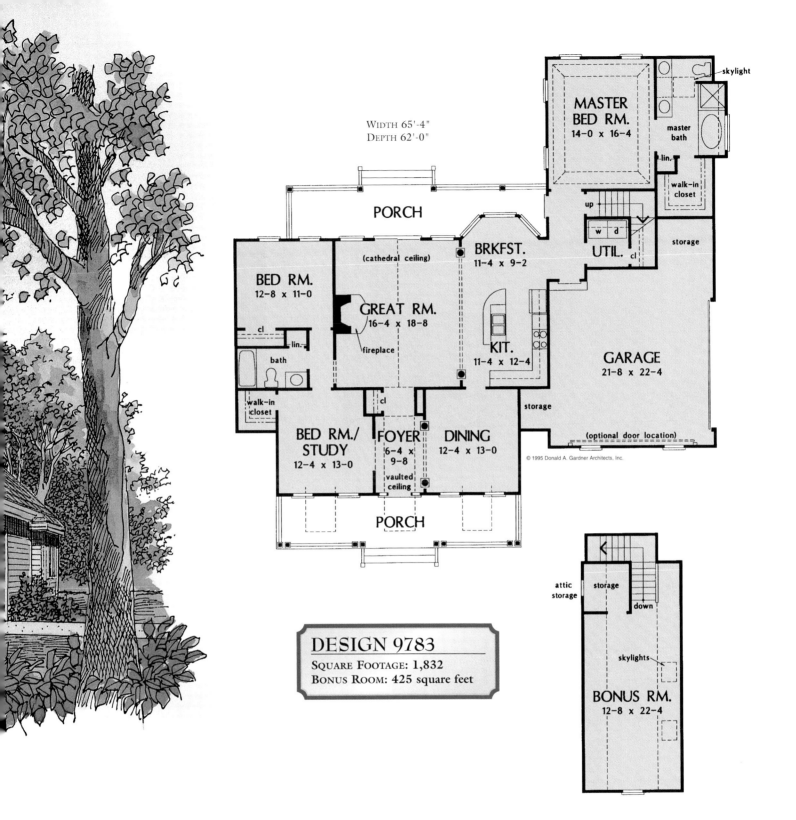

WIDTH 65'-4"
DEPTH 62'-0"

skylight

MASTER BED RM.
14-0 x 16-4

master bath

lin.

walk-in closet

PORCH

up

w d

storage

BRKFST.
11-4 x 9-2

UTIL.

cl

(cathedral ceiling)

BED RM.
12-8 x 11-0

cl

lin.

GREAT RM.
16-4 x 18-8

fireplace

KIT.
11-4 x 12-4

GARAGE
21-8 x 22-4

bath

walk-in closet

cl

BED RM./
STUDY
12-4 x 13-0

FOYER
6-4 x 9-8

vaulted ceiling

DINING
12-4 x 13-0

storage

(optional door location)

© 1995 Donald A. Gardner Architects, Inc.

PORCH

DESIGN 9783

SQUARE FOOTAGE: 1,832
BONUS ROOM: 425 square feet

attic storage

storage

down

skylights

BONUS RM.
12-8 x 22-4

The charm of this home is evident at first glance, but you'll especially appreciate its qualities the moment you step inside. The vaulted foyer ushers guests to the formal dining room and leads back to casual living space. A magnificent great room beckons with a cathedral ceiling and an extended-hearth fireplace, while sliding glass doors, framed by tall windows, provide access to the rear covered porch.

The gourmet kitchen with an island counter enjoys sunlight from the nearby breakfast bay, and leads to a hall with rear porch access. A first-floor main suite features a tray ceiling and a skylit bath with garden tub and a U-shaped walk-in closet. A sizable skylit bonus room above the garage awaits future development. *For similar plans, please see Design 9779 on pages 18-19 and Design 9782 on page 103.*

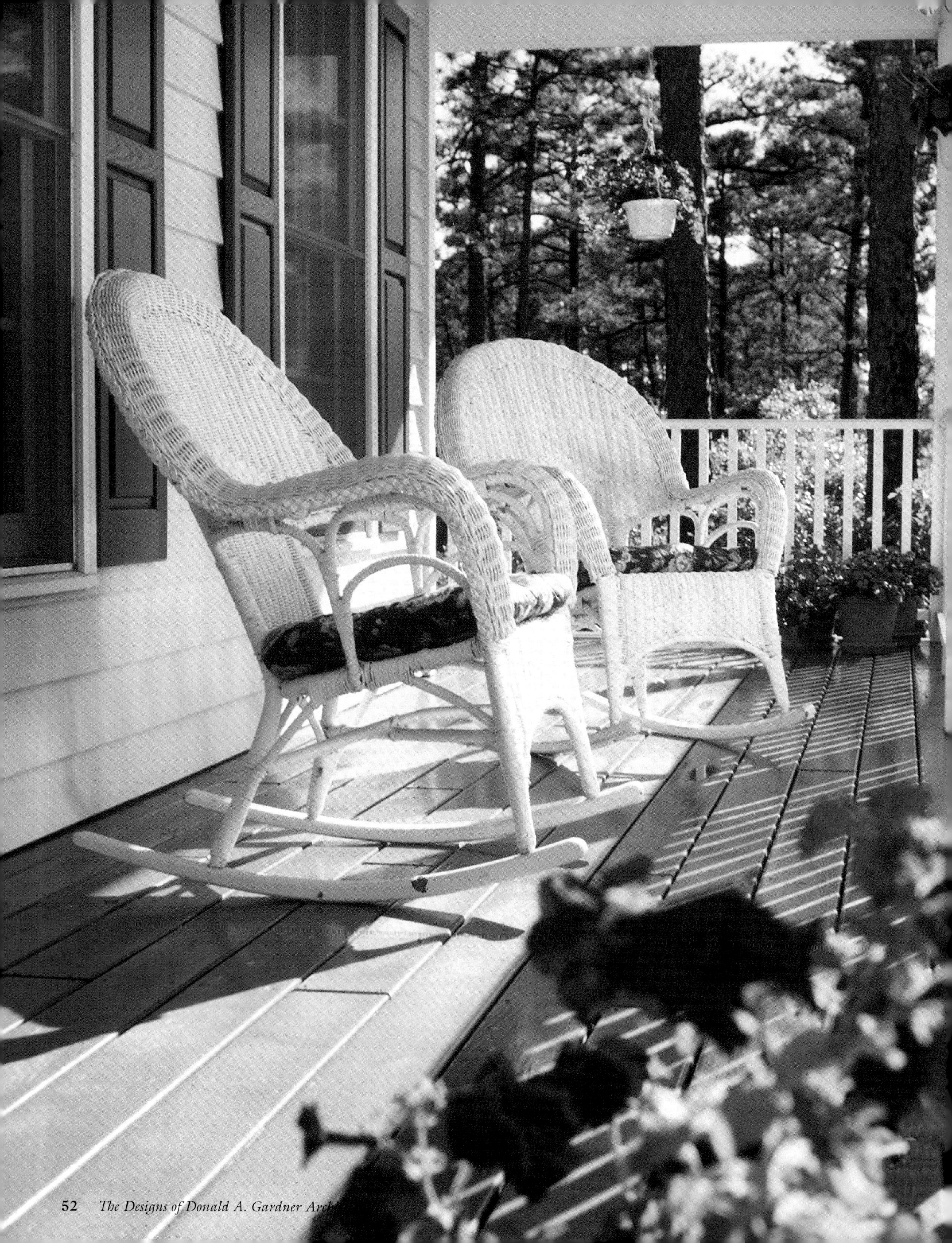

A Passion For Porches

Country homes to wrap around your heart

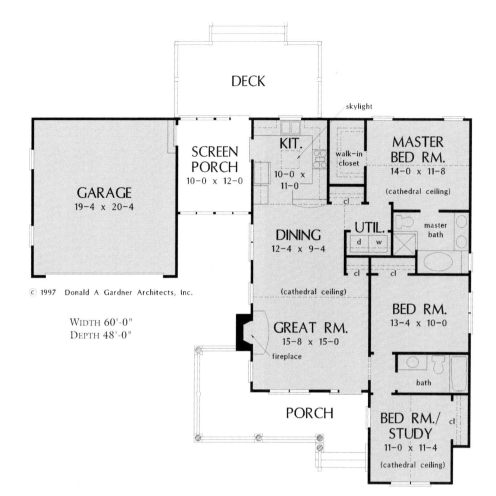

© 1997 Donald A Gardner Architects, Inc.

WIDTH 60'-0"
DEPTH 48'-0"

O pen living spaces allow an easy flow in this gracious country cottage, and vaulted ceilings add volume. The front porch wraps slightly, giving the illusion of a larger home, while a cathedral ceiling maximizes space in the open great room and dining room. The kitchen features a center skylight, breakfast bar and screened porch access. Two bedrooms share a bath up front, while the main suite enjoys a private location to the back of the plan.

DESIGN 7704
SQUARE FOOTAGE: 1,246

THE *Ryley*

B. NATHAN.

© 1997 Donald A. Gardner Architects, Inc.

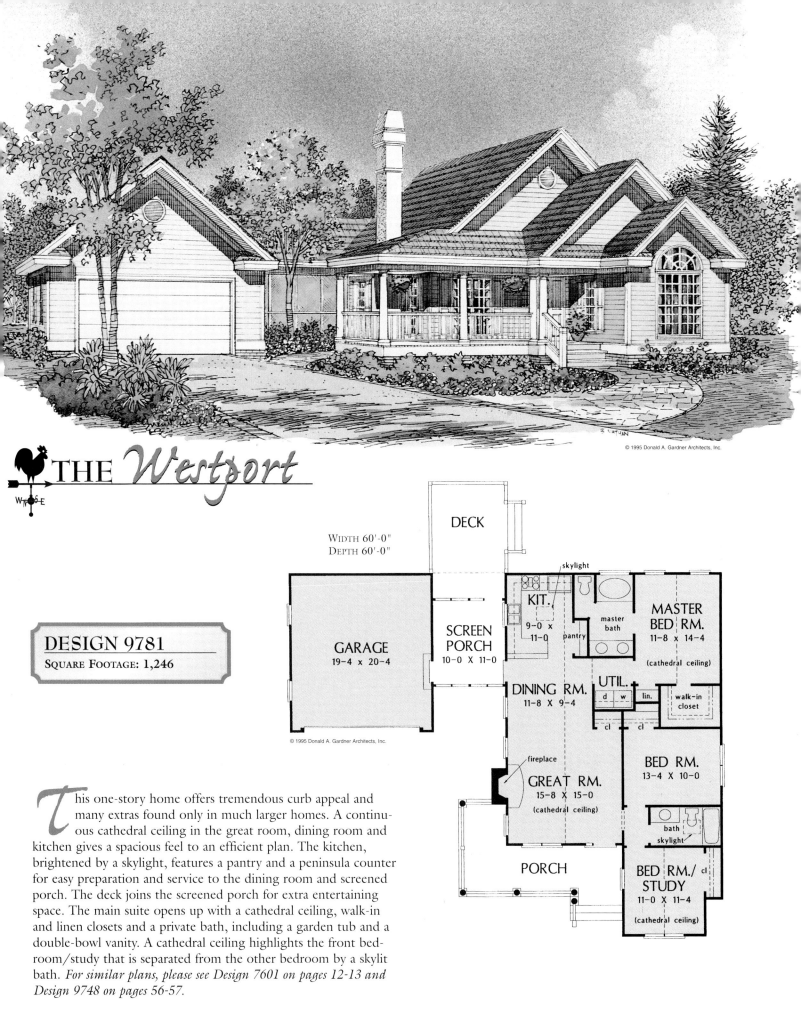

THE *Westport*

W N S E

WIDTH 60'-0"
DEPTH 60'-0"

© 1995 Donald A. Gardner Architects, Inc.

DESIGN 9781
SQUARE FOOTAGE: 1,246

DECK

GARAGE
19-4 x 20-4

SCREEN PORCH
10-0 X 11-0

KIT.
9-0 x 11-0

skylight

master bath

pantry

MASTER BED RM.
11-8 x 14-4
(cathedral ceiling)

DINING RM.
11-8 X 9-4

UTIL.
d w lin.
cl cl

walk-in closet

fireplace

GREAT RM.
15-8 X 15-0
(cathedral ceiling)

BED RM.
13-4 X 10-0

bath
skylight

PORCH

BED RM./ STUDY
11-0 X 11-4
(cathedral ceiling)

cl

© 1995 Donald A. Gardner Architects, Inc.

*T*his one-story home offers tremendous curb appeal and many extras found only in much larger homes. A continuous cathedral ceiling in the great room, dining room and kitchen gives a spacious feel to an efficient plan. The kitchen, brightened by a skylight, features a pantry and a peninsula counter for easy preparation and service to the dining room and screened porch. The deck joins the screened porch for extra entertaining space. The main suite opens up with a cathedral ceiling, walk-in and linen closets and a private bath, including a garden tub and a double-bowl vanity. A cathedral ceiling highlights the front bedroom/study that is separated from the other bedroom by a skylit bath. *For similar plans, please see Design 7601 on pages 12-13 and Design 9748 on pages 56-57.*

THE *Brennan*

*This classic farmhouse design enjoys a wraparound
porch that's perfect for enjoyment of the outdoors.
Distinctive details include sturdy, round columns
acting as a dramatic counterpoint to the more
delicate woodwork of the balustrade and rails.*

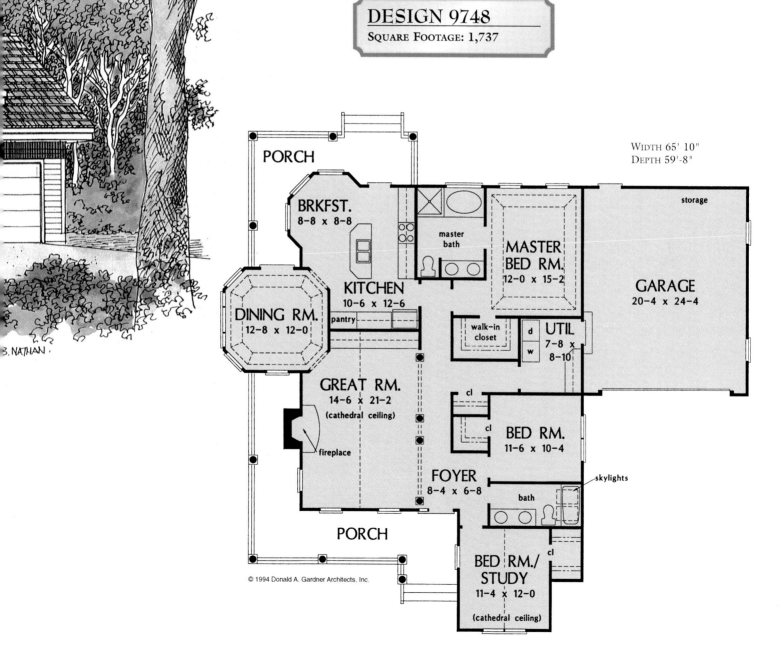

Inviting porches are just the beginning of this lovely country home. To the left of the foyer, a columned entry supplies a classic touch to a spacious great room that features a cathedral ceiling, built-in bookshelves and a fireplace that invites you to share its warmth. An octagonal dining room with a tray ceiling provides a perfect setting for formal occasions. The adjacent kitchen is designed to easily serve both formal and informal areas. It includes an island cooktop and a built-in pantry, with the sunny breakfast area just a step away. The main bedroom, separated from two family bedrooms by the walk-in closet and utility room, offers privacy and comfort. *For similar plans, please see Design 7601 on pages 12-13 and Design 9781 on page 55.*

DESIGN 9748
SQUARE FOOTAGE: 1,737

WIDTH 65' 10"
DEPTH 59'-8"

PORCH

BRKFST.
8-8 x 8-8

master bath

MASTER BED RM.
12-0 x 15-2

storage

GARAGE
20-4 x 24-4

DINING RM.
12-8 x 12-0

KITCHEN
10-6 x 12-6

pantry

walk-in closet

d

w

UTIL
7-8 x 8-10

GREAT RM.
14-6 x 21-2
(cathedral ceiling)

fireplace

cl

cl

BED RM.
11-6 x 10-4

FOYER
8-4 x 6-8

skylights

bath

PORCH

© 1994 Donald A. Gardner Architects, Inc.

cl

BED RM./ STUDY
11-4 x 12-0

(cathedral ceiling)

B. NATHAN

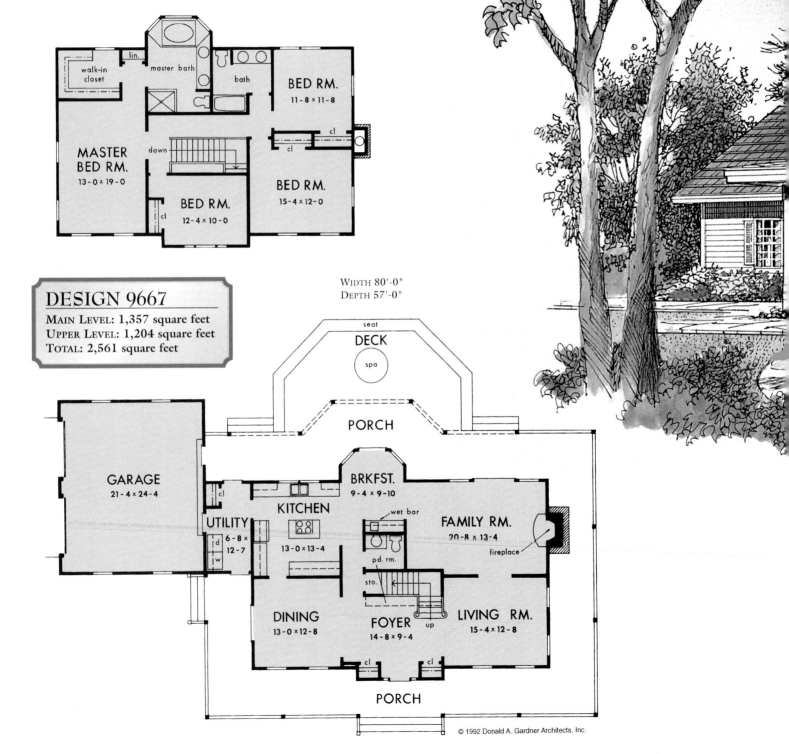

*T*his grand four-bedroom farmhouse with wraparound porch has eye-catching features: a double-gabled roof, a Palladian window at the upper level, an arched window on the lower level and an intricately detailed brick chimney. Entry to the home reveals a generous foyer with direct access to all areas. The living room opens to the foyer and provides a formal entertaining area. The exceptionally large family room allows for more casual living. Look for a fireplace, wet bar and direct access to a porch and deck here. The lavish kitchen boasts a cooking island and serves the dining room, breakfast and deck areas. The main suite on the second level has a large walk-in closet and a bath with a whirlpool tub, a separate shower and a double-bowl vanity. Three additional bedrooms share a full bath.

lin.

walk-in closet

master bath

bath

BED RM.
11-8 x 11-8

cl

cl

MASTER BED RM.
13-0 x 19-0

down

BED RM.
12-4 x 10-0

cl

BED RM.
15-4 x 12-0

DESIGN 9667

MAIN LEVEL: 1,357 square feet
UPPER LEVEL: 1,204 square feet
TOTAL: 2,561 square feet

WIDTH 80'-0"
DEPTH 57'-0"

seat

DECK

spa

PORCH

GARAGE
21-4 x 24-4

BRKFST.
9-4 x 9-10

KITCHEN

UTILITY
6-8 x 12-7

13-0 x 13-4

wet bar

FAMILY RM.
20-8 x 13-4

fireplace

pd. rm.

sto.

DINING
13-0 x 12-8

FOYER
14-8 x 9-4

up

LIVING RM.
15-4 x 12-8

cl

cl

PORCH

© 1992 Donald A. Gardner Architects, Inc.

© 1992 Donald A. Gardner Architects, Inc.

S. NATHAN.

THE *Warrenton*

Arched multi-paned windows and a balustered wraparound porch splash this classic, country exterior with custom style. Abundant windows allow natural light to enter the well-planned interior, while a brick fireplace provides winter warmth.

Country homes to wrap around your heart 59

© 1990 Donald A. Gardner Architects, Inc.   B·NATHAN·

THE *Riverbend*

The simple elegance of this farmhouse design
is enhanced by such formal details as a
Palladian window, capped by a double gable.
Shutters, wood siding and a wraparound
porch add to the country look.

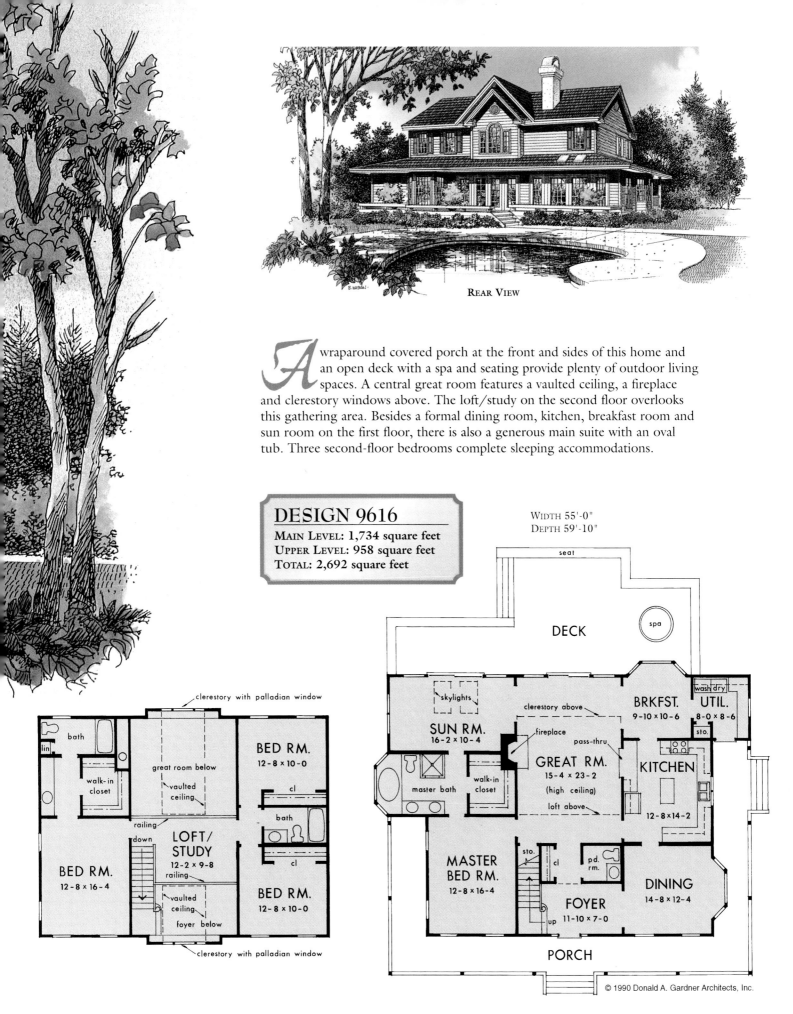

REAR VIEW

A wraparound covered porch at the front and sides of this home and an open deck with a spa and seating provide plenty of outdoor living spaces. A central great room features a vaulted ceiling, a fireplace and clerestory windows above. The loft/study on the second floor overlooks this gathering area. Besides a formal dining room, kitchen, breakfast room and sun room on the first floor, there is also a generous main suite with an oval tub. Three second-floor bedrooms complete sleeping accommodations.

DESIGN 9616

MAIN LEVEL: 1,734 square feet
UPPER LEVEL: 958 square feet
TOTAL: 2,692 square feet

WIDTH 55'-0"
DEPTH 59'-10"

seat

DECK

spa

clerestory with palladian window

bath

lin

walk-in closet

great room below

vaulted ceiling

railing

BED RM.
12-8 × 10-0

cl

bath

cl

down

LOFT/ STUDY
12-2 × 9-8

railing

BED RM.
12-8 × 16-4

vaulted ceiling

foyer below

BED RM.
12-8 × 10-0

clerestory with palladian window

skylights

SUN RM.
16-2 × 10-4

clerestory above

fireplace

master bath

walk-in closet

pass-thru

GREAT RM.
15-4 × 23-2
(high ceiling)

loft above

BRKFST.
9-10 × 10-6

UTIL.
8-0 × 8-6

wash dry

sto.

KITCHEN

12-8 × 14-2

MASTER BED RM.
12-8 × 16-4

sto.

cl

pd. rm.

FOYER
11-10 × 7-0

up

DINING
14-8 × 12-4

PORCH

© 1990 Donald A. Gardner Architects, Inc.

© 1991 Donald A. Gardner Architects, Inc.

THE *Pinckney*

A brick chimney and arch-top windows set in dormers add to this home's country appeal. An abundance of porches and an expansive deck encourage year-round indoor-outdoor living.

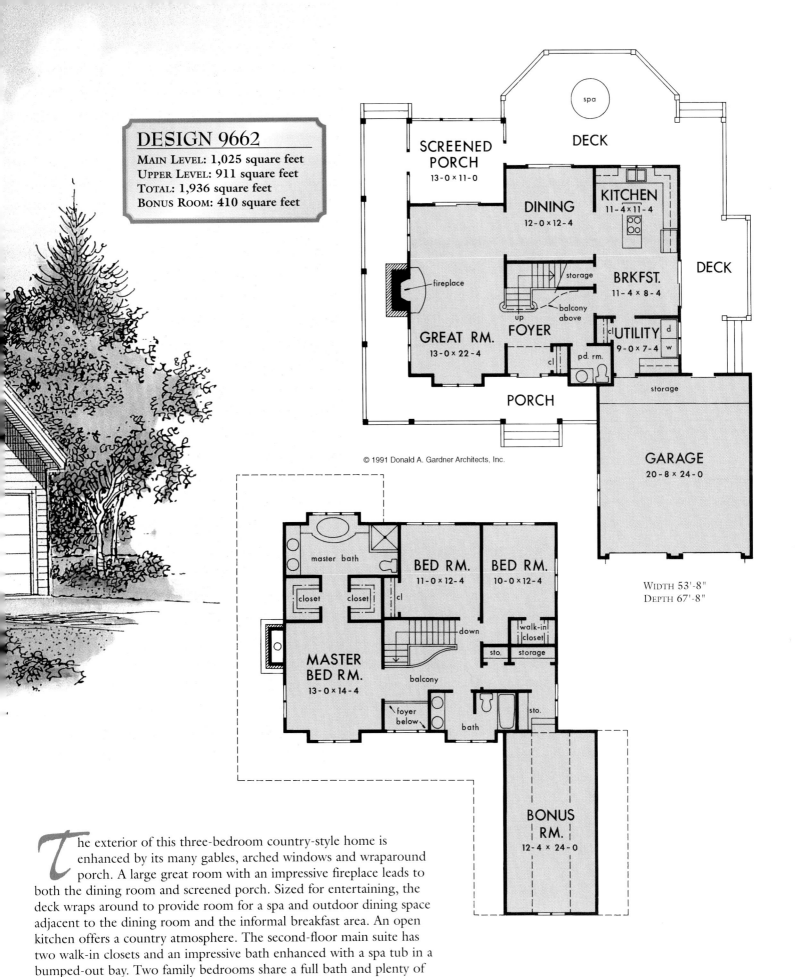

DESIGN 9662

MAIN LEVEL: 1,025 square feet
UPPER LEVEL: 911 square feet
TOTAL: 1,936 square feet
BONUS ROOM: 410 square feet

spa

DECK

SCREENED
PORCH
13-0 × 11-0

DINING
12-0 × 12-4

KITCHEN
11-4 × 11-4

DECK

storage

BRKFST.
11-4 × 8-4

fireplace

balcony
above

up

GREAT RM.
13-0 × 22-4

FOYER

cl

cl

UTILITY
9-0 × 7-4

d

w

pd. rm.

PORCH

storage

GARAGE
20-8 × 24-0

© 1991 Donald A. Gardner Architects, Inc.

master bath

closet

closet

cl

BED RM.
11-0 × 12-4

BED RM.
10-0 × 12-4

walk-in
closet

MASTER
BED RM.
13-0 × 14-4

down

sto.

storage

balcony

foyer
below

bath

sto.

WIDTH 53'-8"
DEPTH 67'-8"

BONUS
RM.
12-4 × 24-0

*T*he exterior of this three-bedroom country-style home is enhanced by its many gables, arched windows and wraparound porch. A large great room with an impressive fireplace leads to both the dining room and screened porch. Sized for entertaining, the deck wraps around to provide room for a spa and outdoor dining space adjacent to the dining room and the informal breakfast area. An open kitchen offers a country atmosphere. The second-floor main suite has two walk-in closets and an impressive bath enhanced with a spa tub in a bumped-out bay. Two family bedrooms share a full bath and plenty of storage. Bonus space over the garage can be developed for future use.

THE *Larson*

With porches front and rear, and a bonus room over the garage, this home is ready to grow with the family. It's a fresh approach to a traditional shape, combining formal architectural details with a floor plan designed for today's families.

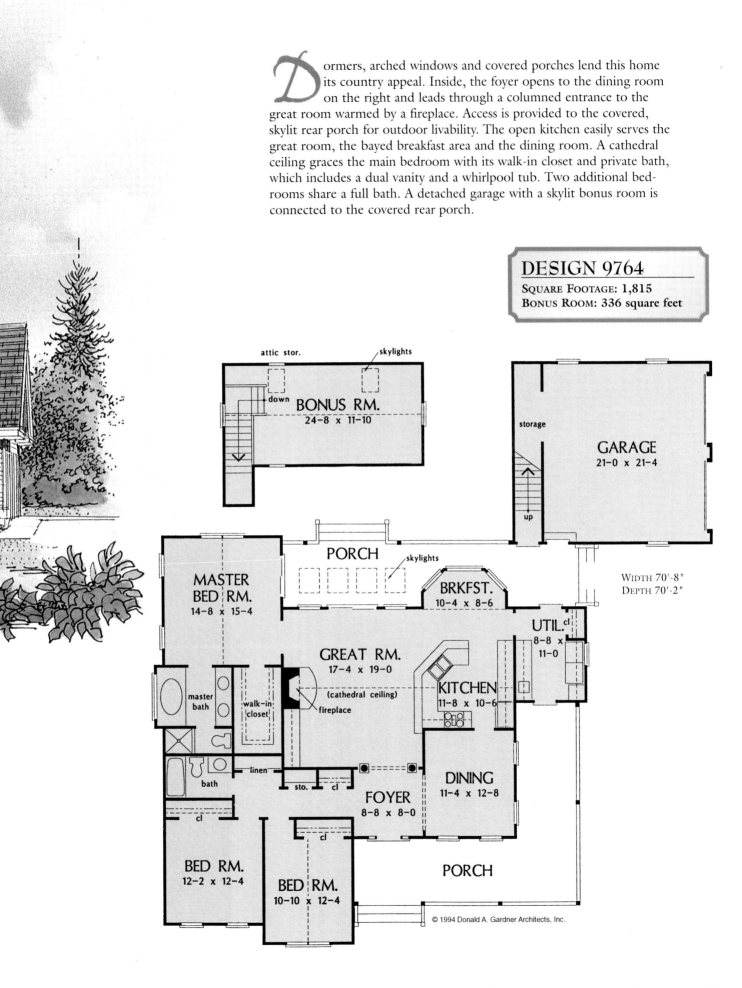

ormers, arched windows and covered porches lend this home its country appeal. Inside, the foyer opens to the dining room on the right and leads through a columned entrance to the great room warmed by a fireplace. Access is provided to the covered, skylit rear porch for outdoor livability. The open kitchen easily serves the great room, the bayed breakfast area and the dining room. A cathedral ceiling graces the main bedroom with its walk-in closet and private bath, which includes a dual vanity and a whirlpool tub. Two additional bedrooms share a full bath. A detached garage with a skylit bonus room is connected to the covered rear porch.

DESIGN 9764
SQUARE FOOTAGE: 1,815
BONUS ROOM: 336 square feet

attic stor.   skylights

BONUS RM.
24-8 x 11-10

down

storage

GARAGE
21-0 x 21-4

up

WIDTH 70'-8"
DEPTH 70'-2"

PORCH   skylights

MASTER BED RM.
14-8 x 15-4

BRKFST.
10-4 x 8-6

UTIL. cl
8-8 x 11-0

GREAT RM.
17-4 x 19-0

(cathedral ceiling)

fireplace

master bath

walk-in closet

KITCHEN
11-8 x 10-6

linen

bath

sto.   cl

FOYER
8-8 x 8-0

DINING
11-4 x 12-8

cl

BED RM.
12-2 x 12-4

BED RM.
10-10 x 12-4

cl

PORCH

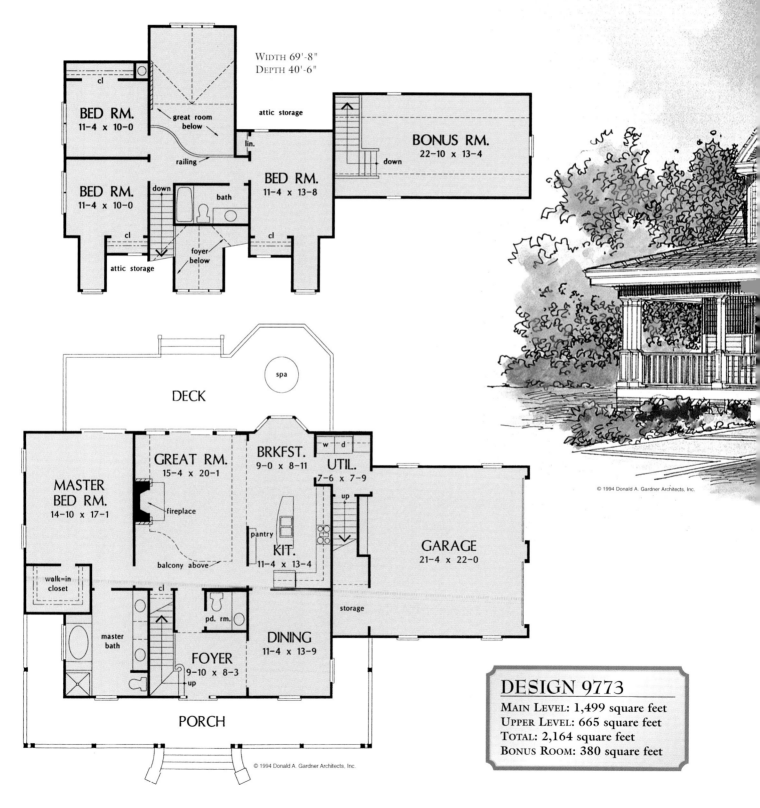

*T*he warm, down-home appeal of this country house is as apparent inside as it is out. A wraparound front porch and a rear deck with a spa provide plenty of space to enjoy the surrounding scenery. Inside, a two-story foyer and a great room give the home an open feel. The great room leads to a breakfast area and an efficient kitchen with an island work area and a large pantry. The main bedroom is situated on the left side of the house for privacy. It features deck access, a large walk-in closet and a bath that includes dual vanities, a whirlpool tub and a separate shower. Three bedrooms, a full bath and bonus space are located upstairs.

WIDTH 69'-8"
DEPTH 40'-6"

cl

BED RM.
11-4 x 10-0

great room below

attic storage

lin.

BONUS RM.
22-10 x 13-4

down

railing

BED RM.
11-4 x 10-0

down

bath

BED RM.
11-4 x 13-8

cl

cl

foyer below

attic storage

spa

DECK

MASTER BED RM.
14-10 x 17-1

GREAT RM.
15-4 x 20-1

fireplace

BRKFST.
9-0 x 8-11

w d

UTIL.
7-6 x 7-9

up

pantry

KIT.
11-4 x 13-4

GARAGE
21-4 x 22-0

balcony above

walk-in closet

cl

pd. rm.

storage

master bath

DINING
11-4 x 13-9

FOYER
9-10 x 8-3

up

PORCH

© 1994 Donald A. Gardner Architects, Inc.

© 1994 Donald A. Gardner Architects, Inc.

DESIGN 9773
MAIN LEVEL: 1,499 square feet
UPPER LEVEL: 665 square feet
TOTAL: 2,164 square feet
BONUS ROOM: 380 square feet

B. NATHAN

THE *Midland*

The twin dormers, Palladian window and central gable of this charming country home work in concert to create a classic architectural statement. Twin pilasters frame a welcoming entry, featuring a paneled door with sidelights.

© 1991 Donald A. Gardner Architects, Inc.

THE *Woodland*

This country estate enjoys plenty of exterior space, perfect for indoor/outdoor activities. Yet for all its down-home appearance, the interior is designed for contemporary family living and entertaining on a grand scale.

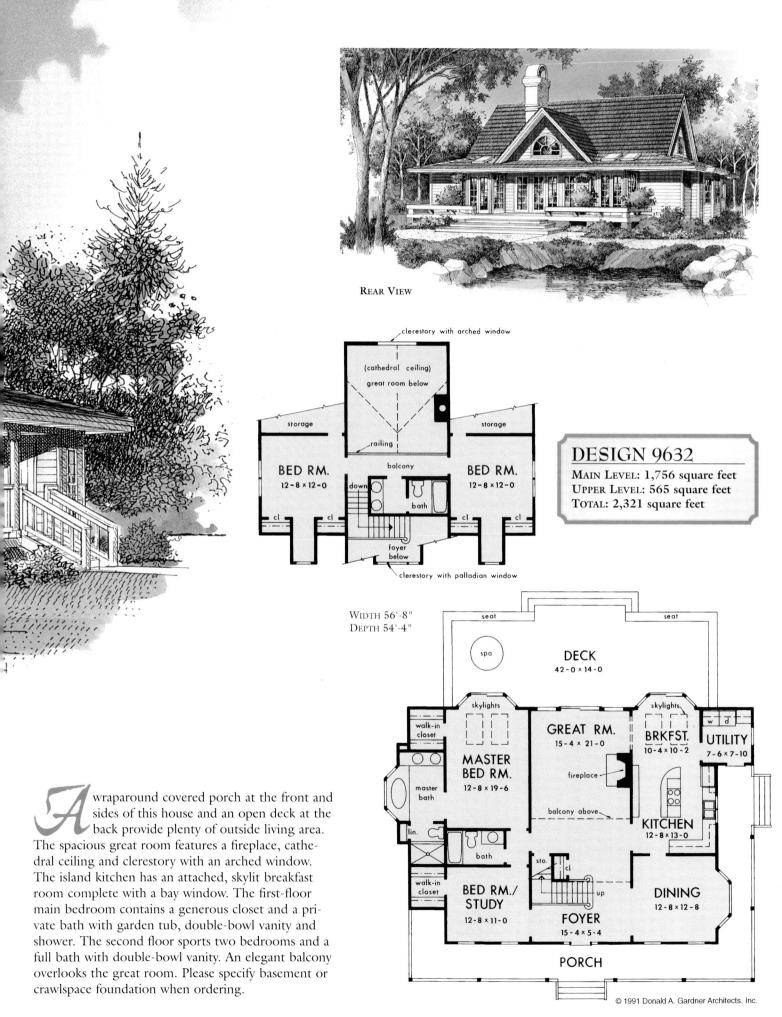

REAR VIEW

clerestory with arched window

(cathedral ceiling)
great room below

storage | storage

railing

balcony

BED RM.
12-8 × 12-0

BED RM.
12-8 × 12-0

down

bath

cl | cl | cl | cl

foyer
below

clerestory with palladian window

DESIGN 9632
MAIN LEVEL: 1,756 square feet
UPPER LEVEL: 565 square feet
TOTAL: 2,321 square feet

WIDTH 56'-8"
DEPTH 54'-4"

seat | seat

spa

DECK
42-0 × 14-0

skylights | skylights

walk-in closet

MASTER
BED RM.
12-8 × 19-6

GREAT RM.
15-4 × 21-0

BRKFST.
10-4 × 10-2

UTILITY
7-6 × 7-10

w d

master bath

fireplace

KITCHEN
12-8 × 13-0

lin.

balcony above

bath

walk-in closet

BED RM./
STUDY
12-8 × 11-0

sto.

cl

up

FOYER
15-4 × 5-4

DINING
12-8 × 12-8

PORCH

© 1991 Donald A. Gardner Architects, Inc.

A wraparound covered porch at the front and sides of this house and an open deck at the back provide plenty of outside living area. The spacious great room features a fireplace, cathedral ceiling and clerestory with an arched window. The island kitchen has an attached, skylit breakfast room complete with a bay window. The first-floor main bedroom contains a generous closet and a private bath with garden tub, double-bowl vanity and shower. The second floor sports two bedrooms and a full bath with double-bowl vanity. An elegant balcony overlooks the great room. Please specify basement or crawlspace foundation when ordering.

© 1991 Donald A. Gardner Architects, Inc.

THE *Morninglory*

*T*his compact design has all the amenities available in larger plans with little wasted space. In addition, a wraparound covered porch, a front Palladian window, dormers and rear arched windows provide exciting visual elements to the exterior. The spacious great room has a fireplace, a cathedral ceiling and clerestory windows. A second-level balcony overlooks this gathering area. The kitchen is centrally located for maximum flexibility in layout and features a pass-through to the great room. Besides the generous main suite with a full bath, there are two family bedrooms located on the second level sharing a full bath that has a double vanity. Please specify basement or crawlspace foundation when ordering.

DESIGN 9621
MAIN LEVEL: 1,325 square feet
UPPER LEVEL: 453 square feet
TOTAL: 1,778 square feet

WIDTH 48'-4"
DEPTH 51'-10"

seat

DECK
41-10 x 13-4

spa

seat

GREAT RM.
15-4 x 19-2

BRKFST.
9-0 x 9-2

wash dry cl

UTILITY
7-8 x 6-8

MASTER
BED RM.
11-4 x 15-6

fireplace

pass-thru

KIT.
12-4 x 12-0

balcony above

cl

walk-in
closet

cl

pd. rm.

DINING
11-4 x 12-8

master
bath

FOYER
9-10 x 7-2

up

PORCH

© 1991 Donald A. Gardner Architects, Inc.

clerestory with windows

great room below
(cathedral ceiling)

storage

railing

BED RM.
11-4 x 10-2

down

BED RM.
11-4 x 10-2

cl

cl

bath

cl

foyer
below

cl

clerestory with palladian window

REAR VIEW

The welcoming charm of this country farmhouse is expressed by its many windows and its covered, wraparound porch. A two-story entrance foyer is enhanced by a Palladian window in a clerestory dormer to allow in natural lighting. A first-floor main suite allows privacy and accessibility. The main bath includes a whirlpool tub, a shower and double-bowl vanity along with a walk-in closet. The first floor features nine-foot ceilings throughout with the exception of the kitchen area, which features an eight-foot ceiling. The second floor provides two additional bedrooms, a full bath and plenty of storage space. A bonus room provides room to grow. Please specify basement or crawlspace foundation when ordering.

DESIGN 9645

MAIN LEVEL: 1,356 square feet
UPPER LEVEL: 542 square feet
TOTAL: 1,898 square feet
BONUS ROOM: 393 square feet

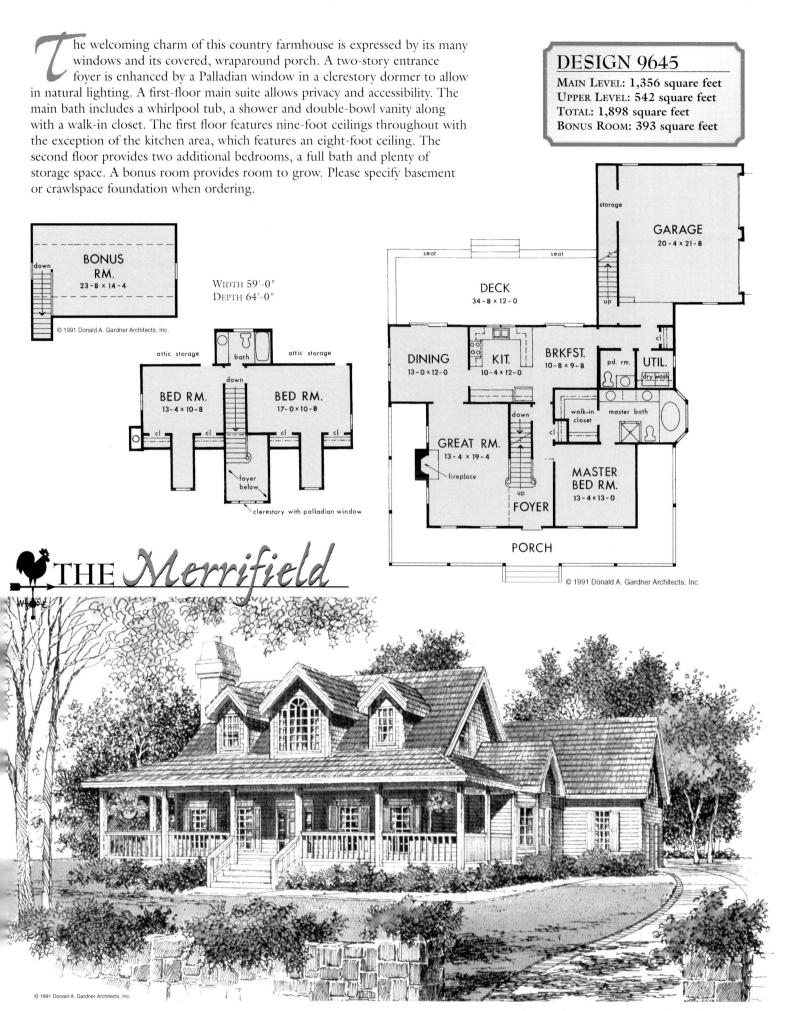

BONUS RM.
23-8 × 14-4

down

© 1991 Donald A. Gardner Architects, Inc.

WIDTH 59'-0"
DEPTH 64'-0"

attic storage   bath   attic storage

BED RM.
13-4 × 10-8

BED RM.
17-0 × 10-8

down

cl   cl   cl   cl

foyer below

clerestory with palladian window

storage

GARAGE
20-4 × 21-8

seat   DECK   seat
34-8 × 12-0

up

DINING
13-0 × 12-0

KIT.
10-4 × 12-0

BRKFST.
10-8 × 9-8

pd. rm.   UTIL.
dry wash

cl

walk-in closet   master bath

GREAT RM.
13-4 × 19-4

down

fireplace

up

MASTER BED RM.
13-4 × 13-0

FOYER

PORCH

© 1991 Donald A. Gardner Architects, Inc.

THE *Merrifield*

Country homes to wrap around your heart   71

© 1991 Donald A. Gardner Architects, Inc.

Look this plan over and you'll be amazed at how much livability can be found in less than 2,000 square feet. A wraparound porch welcomes visitors to the home. Inside lies an enormous great room with a fireplace. To the rear of the home, the breakfast and dining rooms have sliding glass doors to a large deck with room for a spa. The main bedroom contains a walk-in closet and an airy bath with a whirlpool tub. Two bedrooms are found on the second floor, as well as a bonus room over the garage.

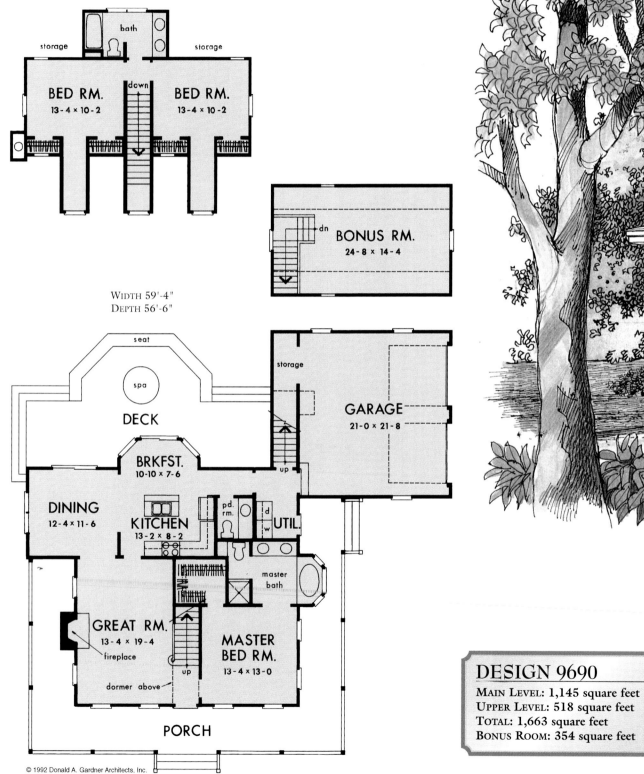

bath

storage

BED RM.
13-4 × 10-2

down

BED RM.
13-4 × 10-2

storage

dn

BONUS RM.
24-8 × 14-4

WIDTH 59'-4"
DEPTH 56'-6"

seat

spa

DECK

storage

GARAGE
21-0 × 21-8

BRKFST.
10-10 × 7-6

up

DINING
12-4 × 11-6

KITCHEN
13-2 × 8-2

pd. rm.

d w

UTIL.

master bath

GREAT RM.
13-4 × 19-4

fireplace

up

MASTER BED RM.
13-4 × 13-0

dormer above

PORCH

© 1992 Donald A. Gardner Architects, Inc.

DESIGN 9690

MAIN LEVEL: 1,145 square feet
UPPER LEVEL: 518 square feet
TOTAL: 1,663 square feet
BONUS ROOM: 354 square feet

© 1992 Donald A. Gardner Architects, Inc.

B. NATHAN

THE *Thackery*

Triple dormers triple the appeal of this inviting country farmhouse. Generous amenities such as double closets in the upstairs bedrooms add to this home's many attractive qualities.

© 1994 Donald A. Gardner Architects, Inc.

B. NATHAN

THE Dobbins

Many shuttered windows fill this comfortable home with the warming light of the outdoors. Classic farmhouse styling captures the heart with its multiple dormers, paneled-door entry and columned porch.

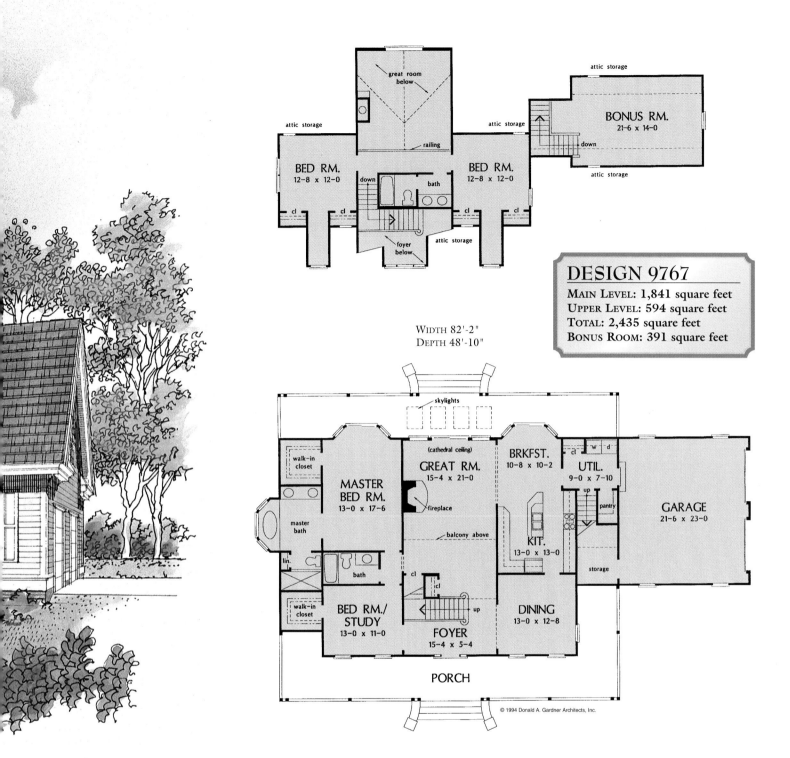

great room
below

attic storage

BONUS RM.
21-6 x 14-0

attic storage

attic storage

down

attic storage

BED RM.
12-8 x 12-0

down

bath

BED RM.
12-8 x 12-0

cl

cl

cl

cl

railing

foyer
below

attic storage

WIDTH 82'-2"
DEPTH 48'-10"

DESIGN 9767

MAIN LEVEL: 1,841 square feet
UPPER LEVEL: 594 square feet
TOTAL: 2,435 square feet
BONUS ROOM: 391 square feet

skylights

walk-in
closet

**MASTER
BED RM.**
13-0 x 17-6

master
bath

lin.

bath

walk-in
closet

**BED RM./
STUDY**
13-0 x 11-0

(cathedral ceiling)

GREAT RM.
15-4 x 21-0

fireplace

balcony above

cl

cl

FOYER
15-4 x 5-4

up

BRKFST.
10-8 x 10-2

w d

cl

UTIL.
9-0 x 7-10

up

pantry

KIT.
13-0 x 13-0

storage

GARAGE
21-6 x 23-0

DINING
13-0 x 12-8

PORCH

© 1994 Donald A. Gardner Architects, Inc.

*A*clerestory window and a quaint covered porch unite to give this upscale home a cottage feel. An inviting glass-paneled entry leads to the grand, two-story foyer, which opens to a formal dining room bright with windows. This home shows its character at the heart of the plan in the great room, where a cathedral ceiling soars above a generous fireplace with an extended hearth, and sliding glass doors lead out to a covered porch with skylights. In the kitchen, oodles of counter and cabinet space along with an island bring out the joy of cooking. The breakfast nook boasts a bumped-out bay that calls in the outdoors and an abundance of natural light. The main bedroom suite features a private bath with a bay-windowed whirlpool tub and an adjoining study with its own walk-in closet. Upstairs, two family bedrooms enjoy a balcony overlook to the great room. A bonus room over the garage awaits further expansion.

REAR VIEW

© 1992 Donald A. Gardner Architects, Inc.

B. NATHAN

THE *Burgess*

This classic country estate boasts a breezeway
to the semi-detached garage, a welcome
addition designed to beat the elements.

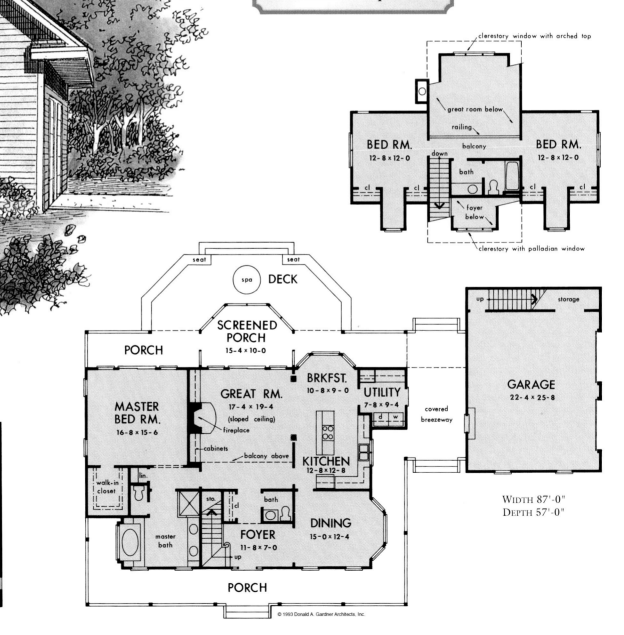

A wraparound covered porch, an open deck with a spa and seating areas, arched windows and dormers enhance the already impressive character of this three-bedroom farmhouse. The entrance foyer and great room with sloped ceilings have Palladian window clerestories to allow natural light to enter. All other first-floor spaces have nine-foot ceilings. The spacious great room boasts a fireplace, cabinets and bookshelves. The kitchen, with a cooking island, is conveniently located between the dining room and the breakfast room with an open view of the great room. A generous main bedroom has plenty of closet space as well as an expansive bath. Bonus room over the garage allows for space to grow.

DESIGN 9702
MAIN LEVEL: 1,618 square feet
UPPER LEVEL: 570 square feet
TOTAL: 2,188 square feet
BONUS ROOM: 495 square feet

clerestory window with arched top

great room below

railing

BED RM.
12-8 × 12-0

balcony

BED RM.
12-8 × 12-0

down

bath

cl

cl

cl

cl

foyer below

clerestory with palladian window

DECK

seat

spa

seat

SCREENED PORCH
15-4 × 10-0

PORCH

BRKFST.
10-8 × 9-0

UTILITY
7-8 × 9-4

up

storage

GARAGE
22-4 × 25-8

MASTER BED RM.
16-8 × 15-6

GREAT RM.
17-4 × 19-4
(sloped ceiling)

fireplace

covered breezeway

cabinets

balcony above

KITCHEN
12-8 × 12-8

d w

walk-in closet

lin.

sto.

cl

bath

master bath

FOYER
11-8 × 7-0

up

DINING
15-0 × 12-4

PORCH

WIDTH 87'-0"
DEPTH 57'-0"

BONUS RM.
15-4 × 29-4

down

© 1993 Donald A. Gardner Architects, Inc.

© 1993 Donald A. Gardner Architects, Inc.

B. NATHAN.

THE *Bentonville*

Spaciousness and attractive amenities earmark this design as a family favorite. A utility room provides direct access to the garage, and an overhead bonus room supplies room for future expansion.

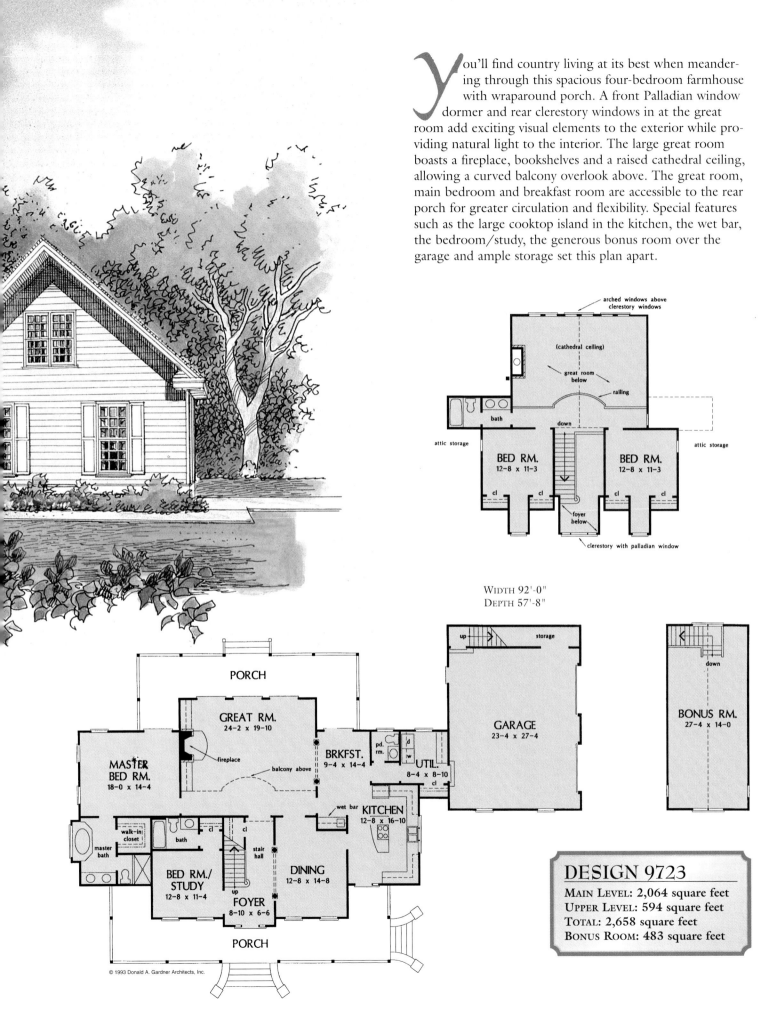

You'll find country living at its best when meandering through this spacious four-bedroom farmhouse with wraparound porch. A front Palladian window dormer and rear clerestory windows in at the great room add exciting visual elements to the exterior while providing natural light to the interior. The large great room boasts a fireplace, bookshelves and a raised cathedral ceiling, allowing a curved balcony overlook above. The great room, main bedroom and breakfast room are accessible to the rear porch for greater circulation and flexibility. Special features such as the large cooktop island in the kitchen, the wet bar, the bedroom/study, the generous bonus room over the garage and ample storage set this plan apart.

arched windows above
clerestory windows

(cathedral ceiling)

great room
below

railing

bath

down

attic storage

attic storage

BED RM.
12-8 x 11-3

BED RM.
12-8 x 11-3

cl   cl

cl   cl

foyer
below

clerestory with palladian window

WIDTH 92'-0"
DEPTH 57'-8"

up   storage

PORCH

GREAT RM.
24-2 x 19-10

fireplace

balcony above

BRKFST.
9-4 x 14-4

pd.
rm.

UTIL.
8-4 x 8-10

GARAGE
23-4 x 27-4

BONUS RM.
27-4 x 14-0

down

MASTER
BED RM.
18-0 x 14-4

cl

wet bar

KITCHEN
12-8 x 16-10

walk-in
closet

bath

master
bath

BED RM./
STUDY
12-8 x 11-4

stair
hall

up

FOYER
8-10 x 6-6

DINING
12-8 x 14-8

PORCH

© 1993 Donald A. Gardner Architects, Inc.

DESIGN 9723
MAIN LEVEL: 2,064 square feet
UPPER LEVEL: 594 square feet
TOTAL: 2,658 square feet
BONUS ROOM: 483 square feet

This grand country farmhouse, with its wraparound porch, offers comfortable living at its finest. The open floor plan is reinforced by a vaulted great room and an entrance foyer with Palladian clerestory windows in dormers above. All spaces are generous in size, with nine-foot ceilings on the first level and eight-foot ceilings on the second. The main suite has beautiful bay windows and a well-designed bath with a cathedral ceiling, His and Hers vanities, a shower, a whirlpool tub and a spacious walk-in closet. The second level includes two large bedrooms, a full bath and plenty of attic storage.

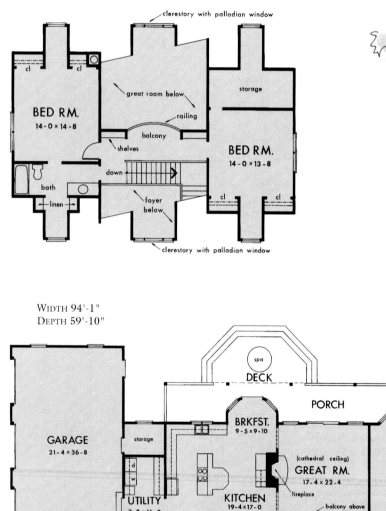

clerestory with palladian window

great room below

railing

balcony

storage

BED RM.
14-0 × 14-8

shelves

BED RM.
14-0 × 13-8

bath

down

linen

foyer below

cl

cl

clerestory with palladian window

WIDTH 94'-1"
DEPTH 59'-10"

spa

DECK

PORCH

GARAGE
21-4 × 36-8

storage

BRKFST.
9-5 × 9-10

(cathedral ceiling)
GREAT RM.
17-4 × 22-4

MASTER
BED RM.
14-0 × 17-0

(cathedral ceiling)
master bath

d   w

UTILITY
7-8 × 11-0

KITCHEN
19-4 × 17-0

fireplace

balcony above

pantry

pd. rm

bath

walk-in closet

sto.

DINING
14-0 × 13-4

(cathedral ceiling)
FOYER
12-8 × 10-8

up

BED RM./
STUDY
14-0 × 11-0

cl

cl

cl

PORCH

© 1993 Donald A. Gardner Architects, Inc.

DESIGN 9708

MAIN LEVEL: 2,238 square feet
UPPER LEVEL: 768 square feet
TOTAL: 3,006 square feet

© 1993 Donald A. Gardner Architects, Inc.

B. NATHAN.

THE *Wynnewood*

The rambling quality of this design gives more than a touch of country style. The bridge between the house and garage provides space for a handy utility room and an extra storage area.

$\mathcal{T}$his gracious farmhouse with its wraparound porch offers a touch of symmetry in a well-defined, open plan. The entrance foyer has a Palladian clerestory window that gives an abundance of natural light to the interior. The vaulted great room furthers this feeling of airiness with a second-floor balcony above and two sets of sliding glass doors leading to the porch out back. The country kitchen with an island countertop, the bayed breakfast nook and the dining room all enjoy nine-foot ceilings. Upstairs, each family bedroom has two closets. A full bath with a double-bowl vanity rests to one side of the hall. For privacy, the main suite occupies the right side of the first floor. With a sitting room and all the amenities of a spa-style bath, this room won't fail to please.

DESIGN 9721

MAIN LEVEL: 2,316 square feet
UPPER LEVEL: 721 square feet
TOTAL: 3,037 square feet
BONUS ROOM: 545 square feet

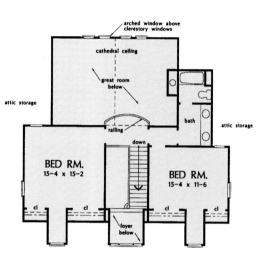

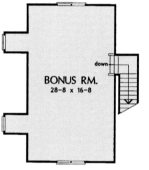

WIDTH 95'-4"
DEPTH 54'-10"

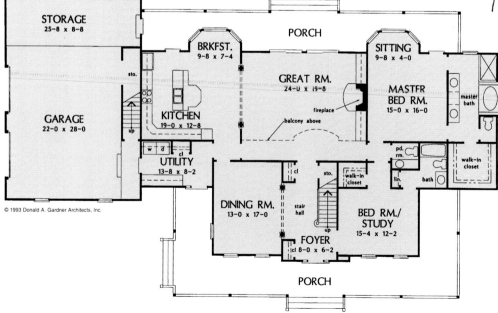

© 1993 Donald A. Gardner Architects, Inc.

© 1993 Donald A. Gardner Architects, Inc.

THE *Forrester*

Sunny dormer windows splash this favorite farmhouse with style, and create a charming facade that's set off by an old-fashioned country porch. Inside, the two-story foyer opens to a spacious interior.

Pitch Perfect

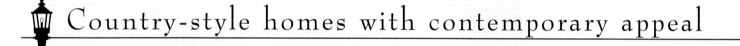

Country-style homes with contemporary appeal

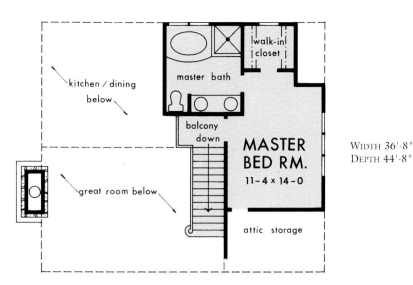

kitchen / dining below

walk-in closet

master bath

balcony down

great room below

MASTER BED RM.
11-4 × 14-0

attic storage

WIDTH 36'-8"
DEPTH 44'-8"

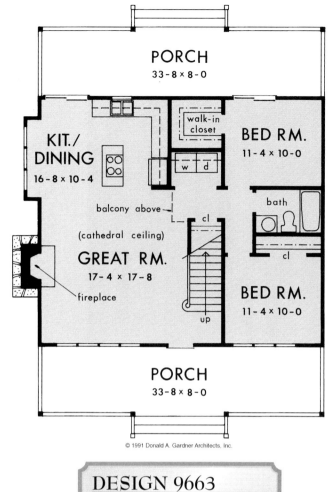

PORCH
33-8 × 8-0

walk-in closet

KIT./ DINING
16-8 × 10-4

BED RM.
11-4 × 10-0

w d

bath

balcony above

cl

GREAT RM.
17-4 × 17-8

(cathedral ceiling)

fireplace

cl

up

BED RM.
11-4 × 10-0

PORCH
33-8 × 8-0

© 1991 Donald A. Gardner Architects, Inc.

A mountain retreat, this rustic home features covered porches front and rear. Open living is enjoyed in a great room and kitchen/dining room combination. Here, a fireplace provides the focal point and a warm welcome that continues into the L-shaped island kitchen. The cathedral ceiling that graces the great room gives an open, inviting sense of space. Two bedrooms—one with a walk-in closet—and a full bath on the first level are complemented by a main suite on the second level, which includes a walk-in closet and deluxe bath. There is also attic storage on the second level. Please specify basement or crawlspace foundation when ordering.

DESIGN 9663

MAIN LEVEL: 1,002 square feet
UPPER LEVEL: 336 square feet
TOTAL: 1,338 square feet

THE *Shady Grove*

© 1991 Donald A. Gardner Architects, Inc.

© 1996 Donald A. Gardner Architects, Inc.

THE *Winston*

*T*his compact plan with a rear garage offers plenty of room for families just starting out as well as empty-nesters scaling down. The great room's cathedral ceiling, combined with the openness of the adjoining dining room and kitchen, create spaciousness beyond this plan's modest square footage. The dining room is enlarged by a bay window, while a picture window with arched top allows ample light into the great room. The efficient U-shaped kitchen leads directly to the garage—convenient for unloading groceries. The main suite features ample closet space and a skylit bath that boasts a double-sink vanity and separate tub and shower.

DESIGN 7749
SQUARE FOOTAGE: 1,372

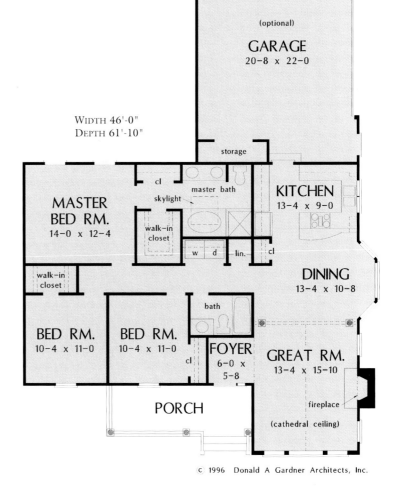

WIDTH 46'-0"
DEPTH 61'-10"

(optional)
GARAGE
20-8 x 22-0

storage

MASTER
BED RM.
14-0 x 12-4

cl

skylight

master bath

walk-in
closet

KITCHEN
13-4 x 9-0

w   d   lin.   cl

walk-in
closet

DINING
13-4 x 10-8

bath

BED RM.
10-4 x 11-0

BED RM.
10-4 x 11-0

FOYER
6-0 x
5-8

cl

GREAT RM.
13-4 x 15-10

fireplace

PORCH

(cathedral ceiling)

© 1996 Donald A Gardner Architects, Inc.

B. NATHAN

THE *Fairethorne*

A recessed covered porch and circle-top windows blend a casual and contemporary look in this country design. Inside, the vaulted ceiling in the great room gracefully arches to receive a center dormer that bathes the room in natural light.

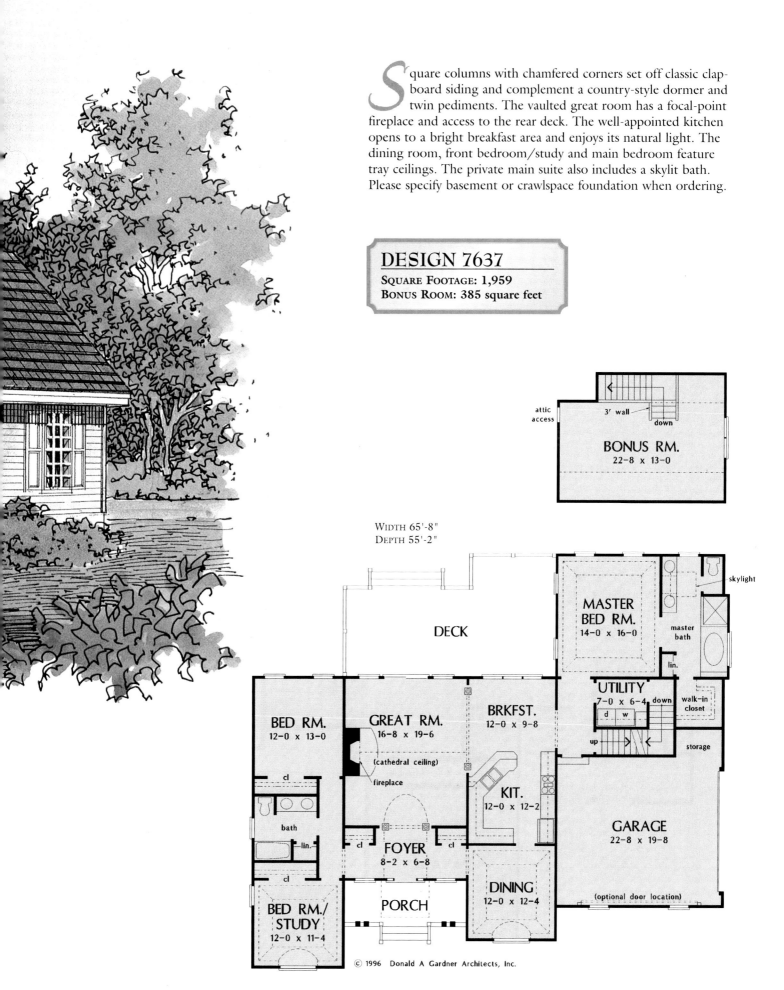

Square columns with chamfered corners set off classic clapboard siding and complement a country-style dormer and twin pediments. The vaulted great room has a focal-point fireplace and access to the rear deck. The well-appointed kitchen opens to a bright breakfast area and enjoys its natural light. The dining room, front bedroom/study and main bedroom feature tray ceilings. The private main suite also includes a skylit bath. Please specify basement or crawlspace foundation when ordering.

DESIGN 7637
SQUARE FOOTAGE: 1,959
BONUS ROOM: 385 square feet

attic access

3' wall   down

BONUS RM.
22-8 x 13-0

WIDTH 65'-8"
DEPTH 55'-2"

DECK

skylight

MASTER BED RM.
14-0 x 16-0

master bath

lin.

BED RM.
12-0 x 13-0

GREAT RM.
16-8 x 19-6

(cathedral ceiling)

fireplace

BRKFST.
12-0 x 9-8

UTILITY
7-0 x 6-4   down

d   w

up

walk-in closet

storage

KIT.
12-0 x 12-2

cl

bath

lin.

cl

FOYER
8-2 x 6-8

cl

GARAGE
22-8 x 19-8

cl

BED RM./ STUDY
12-0 x 11-4

PORCH

DINING
12-0 x 12-4

(optional door location)

© 1996 Donald A Gardner Architects, Inc.

Country-style homes with contemporary appeal   **89**

*R*oundtop windows and an inviting covered porch give this three-bedroom plan irresistible appeal. A two-story foyer provides a spacious feeling to this well-organized open layout. Round columns between the great room and kitchen add to the impressive quality of the plan. Enjoy casual meals from the bay-windowed breakfast nook that overlooks an expansive deck, which promotes casual outdoor living to its fullest. The main suite with a walk-in closet and complete bath is on the second floor along with two additional bedrooms and a full bath. The bonus room over the garage offers room for expansion.

DESIGN 9644

MAIN LEVEL: 943 square feet
UPPER LEVEL: 840 square feet
TOTAL: 1,783 square feet
BONUS ROOM: 323 square feet

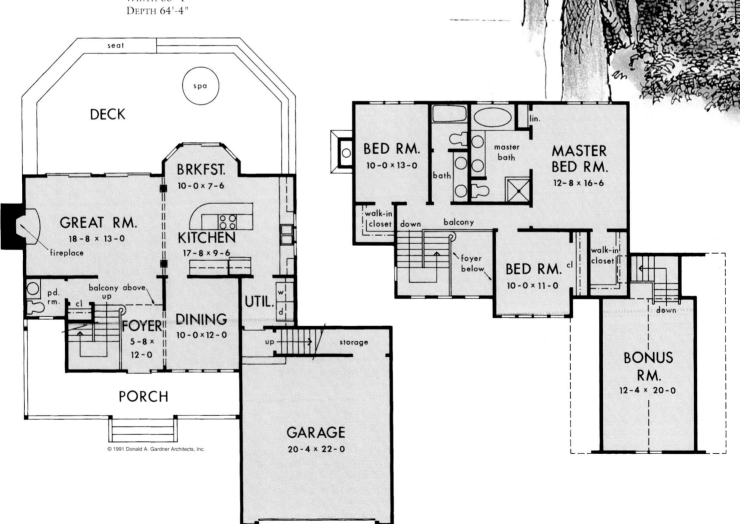

WIDTH 53'-4"
DEPTH 64'-4"

seat

spa

DECK

BRKFST.
10-0 x 7-6

GREAT RM.
18-8 x 13-0

fireplace

KITCHEN
17-8 x 9-6

pd.
rm.

cl

balcony above
up

UTIL.

w
d

FOYER
5-8 x
12-0

DINING
10-0 x 12-0

up

storage

PORCH

© 1991 Donald A. Gardner Architects, Inc.

GARAGE
20-4 x 22-0

BED RM.
10-0 x 13-0

lin.

master
bath

MASTER
BED RM.
12-8 x 16-6

bath

walk-in
closet

down

balcony

foyer
below

BED RM.
10-0 x 11-0

cl

walk-in
closet

down

BONUS
RM.
12-4 x 20-0

B. NATHAN.

THE *Quailcroft* II

A pair of rocking chairs will add a charming touch to this traditional porch. Hanging flower baskets complete the country look.

Country-style homes with contemporary appeal   91

*T*his traditional plan blends a country exterior with a stylish, entirely livable interior plan. The foyer opens to a U-shaped staircase on the right and a bay-windowed formal dining room on the left. Directly ahead is a stunning, two-story great room with centered fireplace and views to the rear property as well as access to a covered porch, perfect for warm summer evenings. A columned archway joins the great room to the kitchen and a bay-windowed breakfast nook, creating an open, spacious living area. The secluded main suite enjoys a raised ceiling and a pampering bath with a windowed garden tub. Two family or guest bedrooms share a full bath on the second floor, which provides a balcony overlook to the family room below. A bonus room offers space for a hobby room or additional storage.

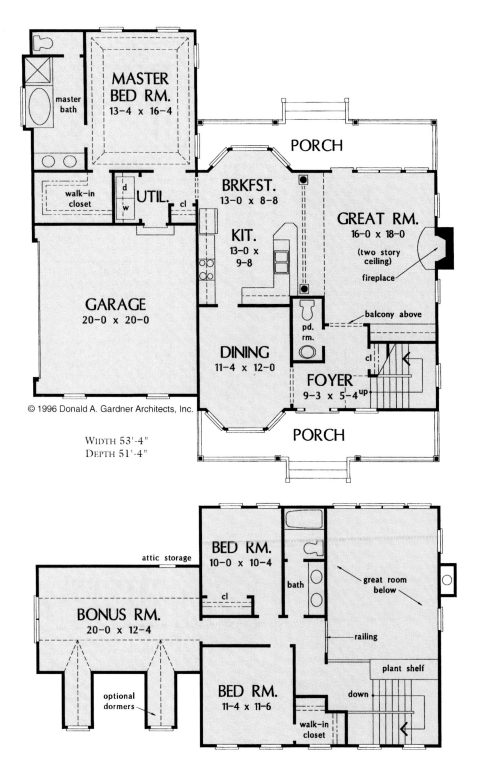

© 1996 Donald A. Gardner Architects, Inc.

WIDTH 53'-4"
DEPTH 51'-4"

DESIGN 7611

MAIN LEVEL: 1,395 square feet
UPPER LEVEL: 502 square feet
TOTAL: 1,897 square feet
BONUS ROOM: 316 square feet

© 1996 Donald A. Gardner Architects, Inc.

B. NATHAN

THE *McColl*

All the charm of a time-tested traditional home stands behind this attractive design. Gables, shutters and a square-columned porch add classic touches and a comfortable scale.

© 1998 Donald A. Gardner, Inc.

B. NATHAN.

THE *Saddlebrook*

Sidelights and an elliptical fanlight add visual interest to the front entrance. The scallop arch above the door is repeated over the porch stairs, to complete the theme.

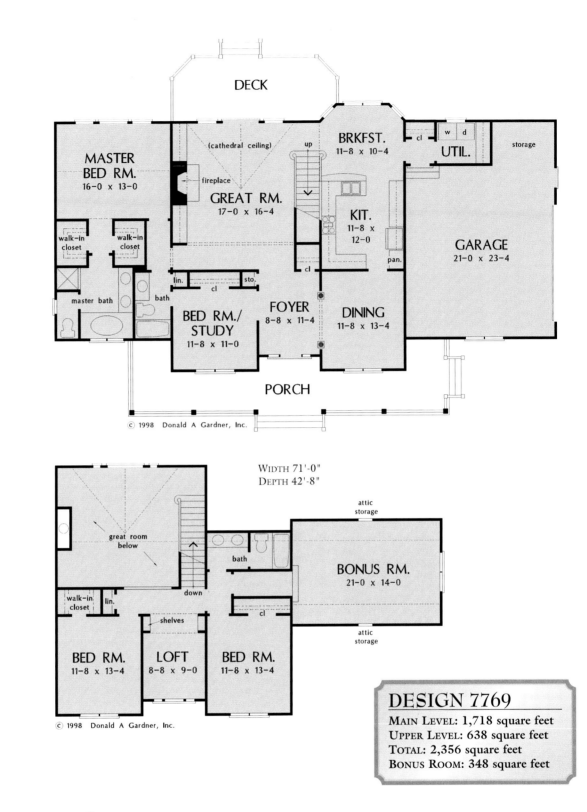

DECK

MASTER
BED RM.
16-0 x 13-0

(cathedral ceiling)

fireplace

GREAT RM.
17-0 x 16-4

up

BRKFST.
11-8 x 10-4

cl

w d

UTIL.

storage

walk-in
closet

walk-in
closet

KIT.
11-8 x
12-0

pan.

GARAGE
21-0 x 23-4

master bath

bath

lin.

cl

sto.

cl

BED RM./
STUDY
11-8 x 11-0

FOYER
8-8 x 11-4

DINING
11-8 x 13-4

PORCH

© 1998 Donald A Gardner, Inc.

WIDTH 71'-0"
DEPTH 42'-8"

attic
storage

great room
below

bath

BONUS RM.
21-0 x 14-0

walk-in
closet

lin.

down

cl

shelves

attic
storage

BED RM.
11-8 x 13-4

LOFT
8-8 x 9-0

BED RM.
11-8 x 13-4

© 1998 Donald A Gardner, Inc.

DESIGN 7769

MAIN LEVEL: 1,718 square feet
UPPER LEVEL: 638 square feet
TOTAL: 2,356 square feet
BONUS ROOM: 348 square feet

*T*win gables and a generous front porch give this graceful farmhouse stature and appeal. Nine-foot ceilings on the first and second floors contribute to the home's overall spaciousness, while vaulted and cathedral ceilings amplify the great room and main bedroom. A rear deck adds outdoor expansion to the great room, which features a fireplace, built-ins, a convenient rear staircase and a balcony overlook. The first-floor main suite enjoys twin walk-in closets and a private bath with a garden tub. A versatile bedroom/study and full bath are nearby. Located upstairs are two family bedrooms, separated by a loft with built-in bookshelves, a liberal bath and bonus room. *For similar plans, please see Design 7650 on pages 8-9 and Design 7656 on pages 96-97.*

THE *Cherryvale*

A pedimented entry, reminiscent of a bygone
era, adds beauty to the front exterior. The
deep front porch was designed to amply
accommodate projecting bay windows.

© 1997 Donald A. Gardner Architects, Inc.

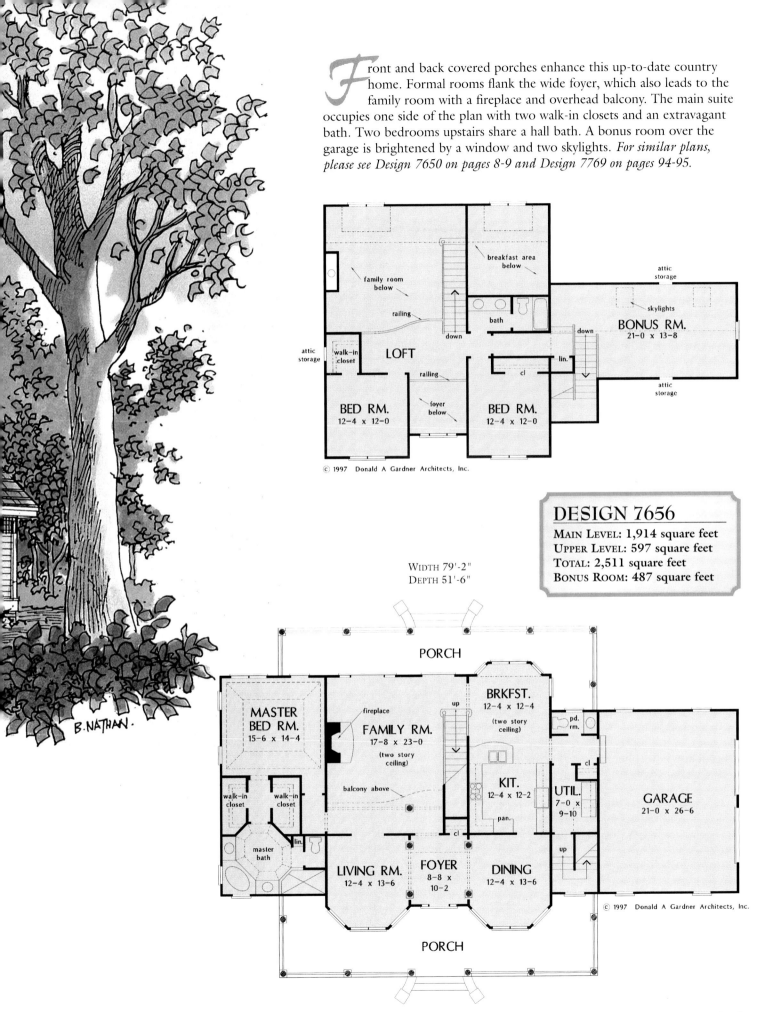

*F*ront and back covered porches enhance this up-to-date country home. Formal rooms flank the wide foyer, which also leads to the family room with a fireplace and overhead balcony. The main suite occupies one side of the plan with two walk-in closets and an extravagant bath. Two bedrooms upstairs share a hall bath. A bonus room over the garage is brightened by a window and two skylights. *For similar plans, please see Design 7650 on pages 8-9 and Design 7769 on pages 94-95.*

family room below

breakfast area below

attic storage

skylights

railing

bath

down

BONUS RM.
21-0 x 13-8

attic storage

LOFT

walk-in closet

down

lin.

cl

attic storage

BED RM.
12-4 x 12-0

railing

foyer below

BED RM.
12-4 x 12-0

© 1997 Donald A Gardner Architects, Inc.

DESIGN 7656
MAIN LEVEL: 1,914 square feet
UPPER LEVEL: 597 square feet
TOTAL: 2,511 square feet
BONUS ROOM: 487 square feet

WIDTH 79'-2"
DEPTH 51'-6"

PORCH

MASTER BED RM.
15-6 x 14-4

fireplace

FAMILY RM.
17-8 x 23-0
(two story ceiling)

up

BRKFST.
12-4 x 12-4

(two story ceiling)

pd. rm.

cl

GARAGE
21-0 x 26-6

walk-in closet

walk-in closet

balcony above

KIT.
12-4 x 12-2

UTIL.
7-0 x 9-10

lin.

master bath

pan.

cl

LIVING RM.
12-4 x 13-6

FOYER
8-8 x 10-2

DINING
12-4 x 13-6

up

© 1997 Donald A Gardner Architects, Inc.

B.NATHAN.

PORCH

Country-style homes with contemporary appeal **97**

© 1999 Donald A. Gardner, Inc.

B. NAT

THE *Northwyke*

A welcoming front porch encourages family and
friends to enter into this fine Craftsman-style home.
A mixture of shingles, gables and columns inspires
a sense of the past and adds to the character and
charm of this very modern design.

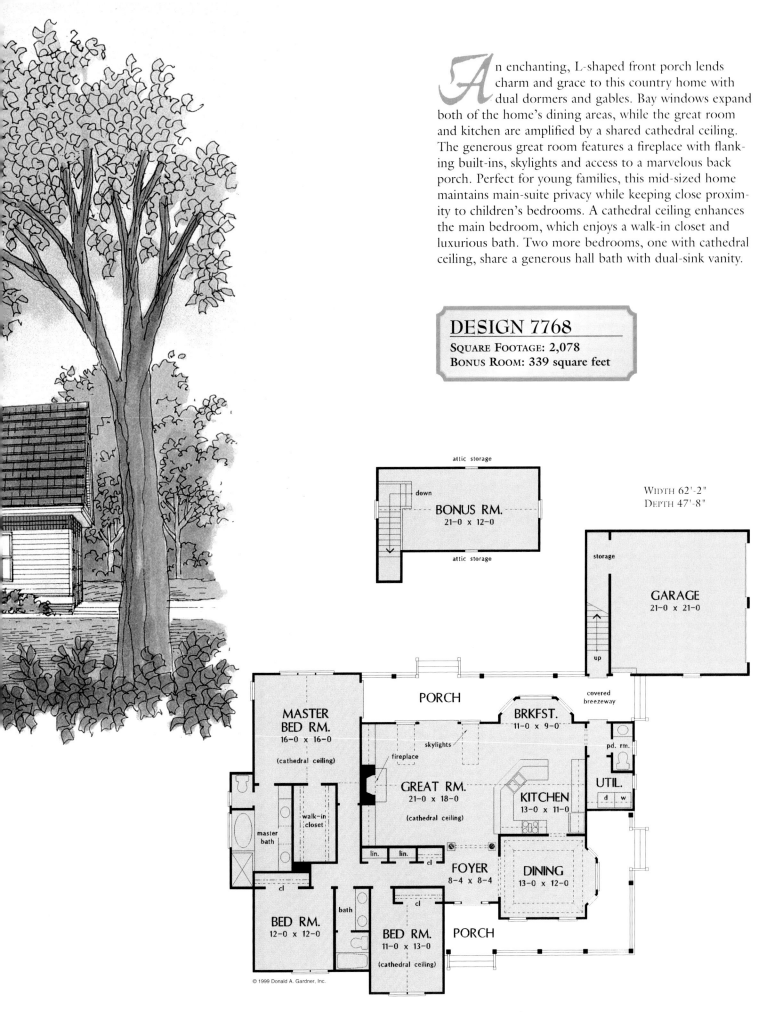

An enchanting, L-shaped front porch lends charm and grace to this country home with dual dormers and gables. Bay windows expand both of the home's dining areas, while the great room and kitchen are amplified by a shared cathedral ceiling. The generous great room features a fireplace with flanking built-ins, skylights and access to a marvelous back porch. Perfect for young families, this mid-sized home maintains main-suite privacy while keeping close proximity to children's bedrooms. A cathedral ceiling enhances the main bedroom, which enjoys a walk-in closet and luxurious bath. Two more bedrooms, one with cathedral ceiling, share a generous hall bath with dual-sink vanity.

DESIGN 7768

SQUARE FOOTAGE: 2,078
BONUS ROOM: 339 square feet

WIDTH 62'-2"
DEPTH 47'-8"

attic storage

down

BONUS RM.
21-0 x 12-0

attic storage

storage

GARAGE
21-0 x 21-0

up

PORCH

covered breezeway

BRKFST.
11-0 x 9-0

MASTER BED RM.
16-0 x 16-0

(cathedral ceiling)

skylights

fireplace

pd. rm.

walk-in closet

GREAT RM.
21-0 x 18-0

(cathedral ceiling)

KITCHEN
13-0 x 11-0

UTIL.

d   w

master bath

lin.   lin.

cl

FOYER
8-4 x 8-4

DINING
13-0 x 12-0

cl

bath

BED RM.
12-0 x 12-0

cl

BED RM.
11-0 x 13-0

(cathedral ceiling)

PORCH

© 1999 Donald A. Gardner, Inc.

© 1997 Donald A. Gardner Architects, Inc.

THE *Jasmine*

The wide covered porch of this delightful design
evokes memories of sipping lemonade on a warm
afternoon or stargazing on a balmy night.
The interior is equally enchanting.

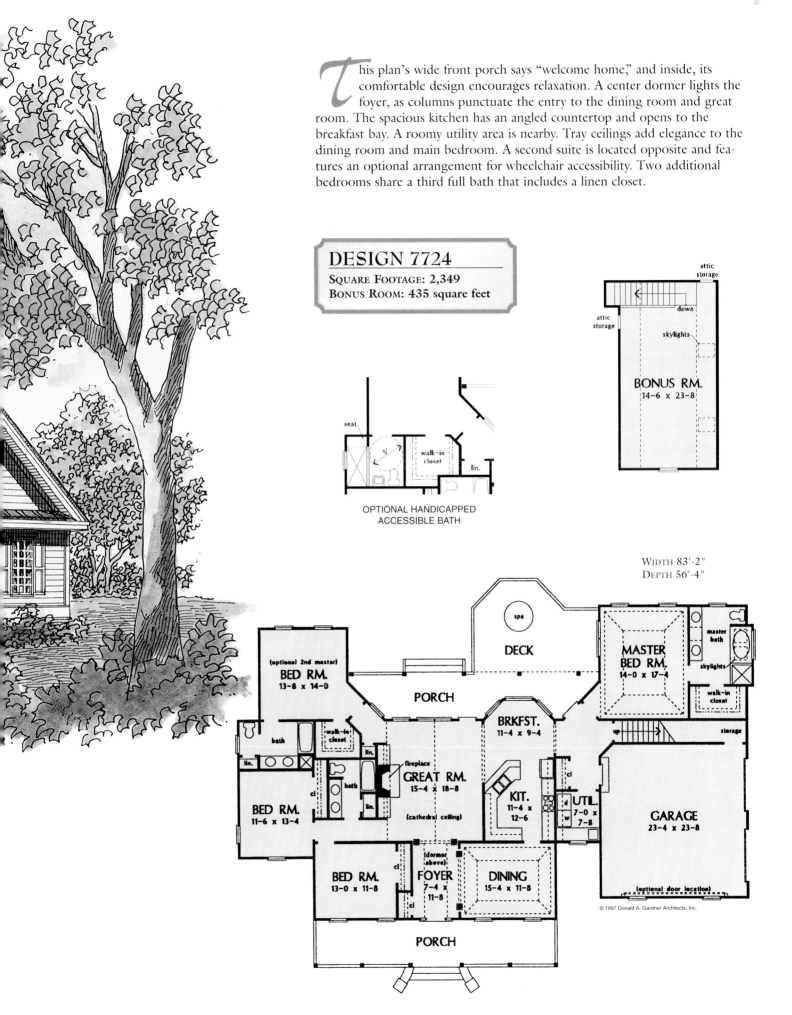

This plan's wide front porch says "welcome home," and inside, its comfortable design encourages relaxation. A center dormer lights the foyer, as columns punctuate the entry to the dining room and great room. The spacious kitchen has an angled countertop and opens to the breakfast bay. A roomy utility area is nearby. Tray ceilings add elegance to the dining room and main bedroom. A second suite is located opposite and features an optional arrangement for wheelchair accessibility. Two additional bedrooms share a third full bath that includes a linen closet.

DESIGN 7724
SQUARE FOOTAGE: 2,349
BONUS ROOM: 435 square feet

attic storage

attic storage

down

skylights

BONUS RM.
14-6 x 23-8

seat

walk-in closet

lin.

OPTIONAL HANDICAPPED
ACCESSIBLE BATH

WIDTH 83'-2"
DEPTH 56'-4"

spa

DECK

master bath

(optional 2nd master)
BED RM.
13-8 x 14-0

MASTER
BED RM.
14-0 x 17-4

skylights

PORCH

BRKFST.
11-4 x 9-4

walk-in closet

bath

walk-in closet

lin.

storage

lin.

fireplace

GREAT RM.
15-4 x 18-8

KIT.
11-4 x 12-6

UTIL.
7-0 x 7-8

GARAGE
23-4 x 23-8

BED RM.
11-6 x 13-4

bath

cl

lin.

(cathedral ceiling)

cl

BED RM.
13-0 x 11-8

cl

(dormer above)

FOYER
7-4 x 11-8

DINING
15-4 x 11-8

(optional door location)

cl

© 1997 Donald A. Gardner Architects, Inc.

PORCH

This exciting three-bedroom country home overflows with amenities. Traditional details such as columns, cathedral ceilings and open living areas combine to create the ideal floor plan for today's active family lifestyle. The spacious great room features built-in cabinets and a fireplace; the cathedral ceiling continues into the adjoining screened porch. An efficient kitchen with a food preparation island is conveniently grouped with the great room, the dining room and the skylit breakfast area for the cook who enjoys visiting while preparing meals. A private main bedroom features a cathedral ceiling, a large walk-in closet and a relaxing bath with a skylit whirlpool tub and a separate shower. Two secondary bedrooms share a full bath at the opposite end of the home.

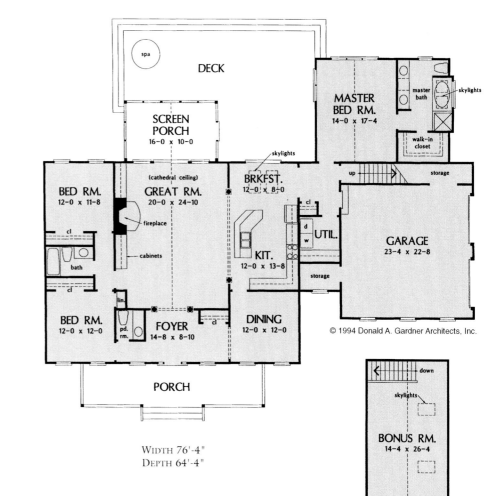

© 1994 Donald A. Gardner Architects, Inc.

WIDTH 76'-4"
DEPTH 64'-4"

DESIGN 9738

SQUARE FOOTAGE: 2,136
BONUS ROOM: 405 square feet

THE *Tamassee*

B. NATHAN
© 1994 Donald A. Gardner Architects, Inc.

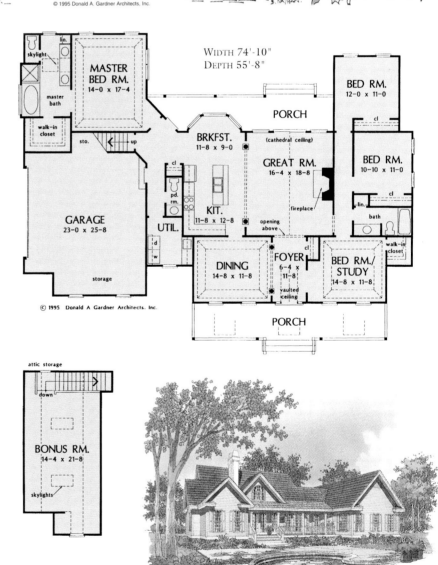

THE *Calhoun*

*E*xciting volumes and nine-foot ceilings add elegance to a comfortable, open plan, while secluded bedrooms are pleasant retreats in this home. Sunlight fills the airy foyer from a vaulted dormer and streams into the great room. A formal dining room, delineated from the foyer by columns, features a tray ceiling. Hosts whose guests always end up in the kitchen will enjoy entertaining here with only columns to separate them from the great room. Secondary bedrooms share a full bath, complete with a linen closet. The front bedroom doubles as a study for extra flexibility and is accented by a tray ceiling. The main suite is highlighted by a tray ceiling and a spacious bath with a walk-in closet. *For similar plans, please see Design 9779 on pages 18-19 and Design 9783 on pages 50-51.*

WIDTH 74'-10"
DEPTH 55'-8"

skylight

MASTER BED RM.
14-0 x 17-4

master bath

walk-in closet

sto.   up

GARAGE
23-0 x 25-8

storage

© 1995 Donald A Gardner Architects. Inc.

BRKFST.
11-8 x 9-0

KIT.
11-8 x 12-8

UTIL.

cl

pd. rm.

d
w

PORCH

(cathedral ceiling)

GREAT RM.
16-4 x 18-8

fireplace

opening above

DINING
14-8 x 11-8

FOYER
6-4 x 11-8

vaulted ceiling

BED RM./ STUDY
14-8 x 11-8

BED RM.
12-0 x 11-0

cl

BED RM.
10-10 x 11-0

cl

lin.

bath

walk-in closet

PORCH

attic storage

down

BONUS RM.
14-4 x 21-8

skylights

DESIGN 9782

SQUARE FOOTAGE: 2,192
BONUS ROOM: 390 square feet

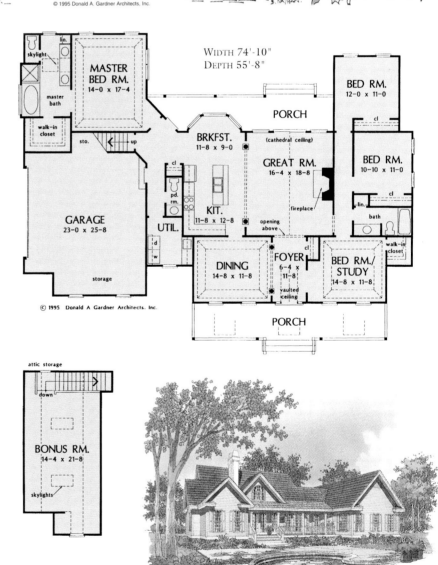

REAR VIEW

Country-style homes with contemporary appeal **103**

THE *Dunwood*

This lovely country design features a welcoming wide porch and plenty of windows to provide the interior with natural light. Planters and hanging flower baskets add color and charm.

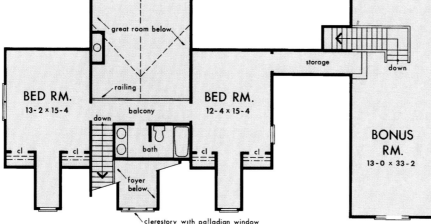

*T*his open country plan boasts front and rear covered porches and a bonus room for future expansion. The entrance foyer with a sloped ceiling has a Palladian window clerestory to allow natural light in. The spacious great room has a fireplace, cathedral ceiling and a clerestory with arched windows. The second-floor balcony overlooks the great room. A U-shaped kitchen provides the ideal layout for food preparation. For flexibility, access is provided to the bonus room from both the first and second floors.

DESIGN 9707

MAIN LEVEL: 1,632 square feet
UPPER LEVEL: 669 square feet
TOTAL: 2,301 square feet
BONUS ROOM: 528 square feet

WIDTH 72'-6"
DEPTH 46'-10"

PORCH

GREAT RM.
15-4 × 19-2
fireplace
(cathedral ceiling)
balcony above

MASTER BED RM.
13-2 × 19-2

BRKFST.
9-10 × 11-10

KIT.
10-10 × 16-4

up
cl
storage

wet bar
sto.
pantry

d   w

walk-in closet

GARAGE
21-8 × 21-0

cl
pd. rm

master bath

FOYER
10-0 × 7-4
up

DINING
12-4 × 12-8

PORCH

© 1993 Donald A. Gardner Architects, Inc.

clerestory with arched window

great room below

railing
balcony

BED RM.
13-2 × 15-4

BED RM.
12-4 × 15-4

storage

down

down
cl   cl
bath
cl   cl

foyer below

BONUS RM.
13-0 × 33-2

clerestory with palladian window

B. NATHAN
© 1993 Donald A. Gardner Architects, Inc.

© 1992 Donald A. Gardner Architects, Inc.

THE *Riverside*

A covered breezeway provides convenient passage from the house to the garage, and to a spacious rear deck with room for a spa tub. A sunny bay window floods the dining room with natural light.

With an elegant but casual exterior, this four-bedroom farmhouse celebrates sunlight with a Palladian window and triple dormers, a skylit screened porch and a rear arched window. The clerestory window in the two-story foyer throws natural light across the loft to the great room, with a fireplace and a cathedral ceiling. The center island kitchen and the breakfast area open to the great room through an elegant colonnade. The first-floor main suite is a calm retreat with its own access to the screened porch through a bay area—and a luxurious bath awaits with a garden tub, dual lavatories and a separate shower. Upstairs, two family bedrooms offer plush amenities: a skylight, a private bath and a dormer window in each room.

DESIGN 9712

MAIN LEVEL: 1,766 square feet
UPPER LEVEL: 670 square feet
TOTAL: 2,436 square feet

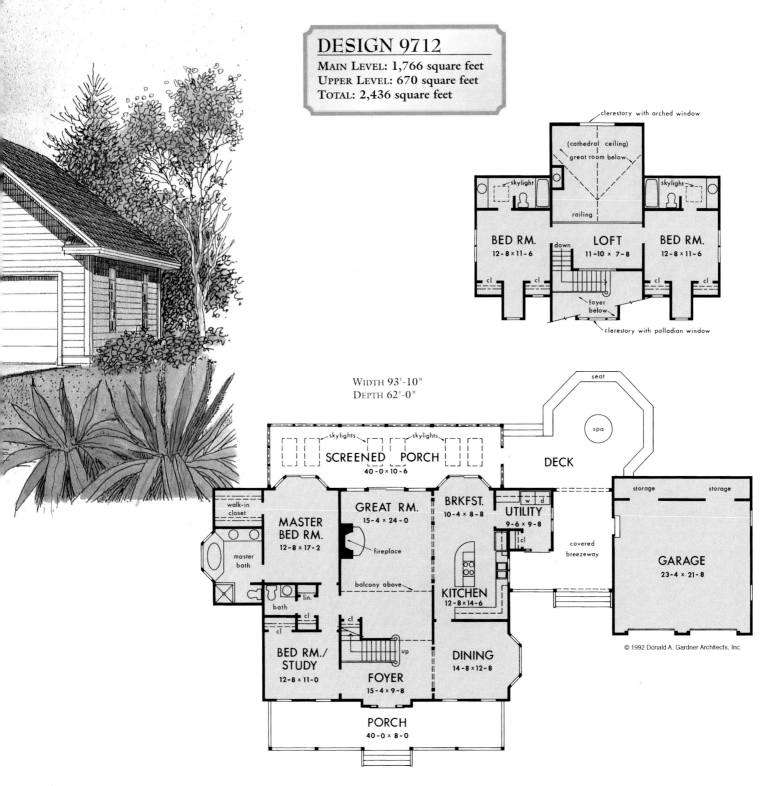

WIDTH 93'-10"
DEPTH 62'-0"

© 1992 Donald A. Gardner Architects, Inc.

© 1998 Donald A. Gardner, Inc.

THE *Silverleaf*

Special details enhance the roofline of this gracious country estate. Gabled dormers with attractive arch-top windows flank a central pediment with an elliptical accent light.

With a front porch perfect for sipping lemonade with friends and neighbors, this charming country estate is a welcome retreat with plenty of room for everyone. Marked by columns, the formal living and dining rooms are positioned up front, while the family gathering areas are open and casual at the back. The vaulted foyer and gener-ous great room with cathedral ceiling receive added drama from a second-floor balcony that overlooks both. The first-floor main suite features an elegant tray ceiling, and a bayed sitting area offers a private spot for relaxation. Upstairs, two bedrooms, both with cathedral ceilings, two full baths and an enormous bonus room provide plenty of room for the family.

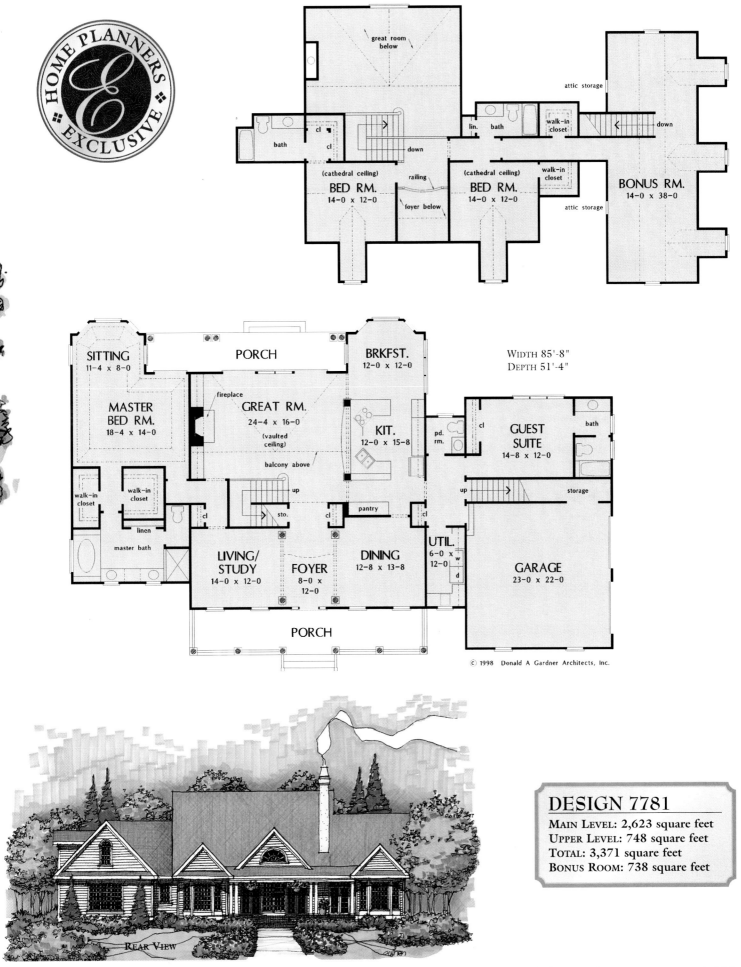

HOME PLANNERS EXCLUSIVE

Upper Level

great room below

attic storage

BED RM.
14-0 x 12-0
(cathedral ceiling)

bath

cl

cl

down

railing

foyer below

lin.

bath

walk-in closet

(cathedral ceiling)

BED RM.
14-0 x 12-0

walk-in closet

attic storage

down

BONUS RM.
14-0 x 38-0

Main Level

SITTING
11-4 x 8-0

PORCH

BRKFST.
12-0 x 12-0

WIDTH 85'-8"
DEPTH 51'-4"

MASTER
BED RM.
18-4 x 14-0

fireplace

GREAT RM.
24-4 x 16-0
(vaulted ceiling)

balcony above

KIT.
12-0 x 15-8

pd. rm.

cl

GUEST
SUITE
14-8 x 12-0

bath

walk-in closet

walk-in closet

up

up

storage

linen

cl

sto.

pantry

cl

cl

master bath

LIVING/
STUDY
14-0 x 12-0

FOYER
8-0 x 12-0

DINING
12-8 x 13-8

UTIL.
6-0 x 12-0

w
d

GARAGE
23-0 x 22-0

PORCH

© 1998 Donald A Gardner Architects, Inc.

REAR VIEW

DESIGN 7781
MAIN LEVEL: 2,623 square feet
UPPER LEVEL: 748 square feet
TOTAL: 3,371 square feet
BONUS ROOM: 738 square feet

THE *Brookhaven*

The outstanding facade of this home features enduring elements such as dormers, multi-paned windows and a covered porch supported by twin sets of pilasters. The gentle, scallop curve above the porch is repeated above the door, adding architectural interest.

Graceful arches adorn an inviting front porch, while a lovely trio of dormers adds charm and appeal to this classic country home. A two-story ceiling tops the foyer where a dramatic, curved staircase leads to a second-floor balcony, which overlooks both foyer and family room. Both the living and family rooms feature interior columns and fireplaces with flanking built-ins. The first-floor main suite is enhanced by an adjoining sitting room, a fireplace, two walk-in closets and a sumptuous bath. One of the three upstairs bedrooms enjoys its own private bath and walk-in closet. A spacious bonus room, accessed from the kitchen, makes a great recreation room or playroom for the kids.

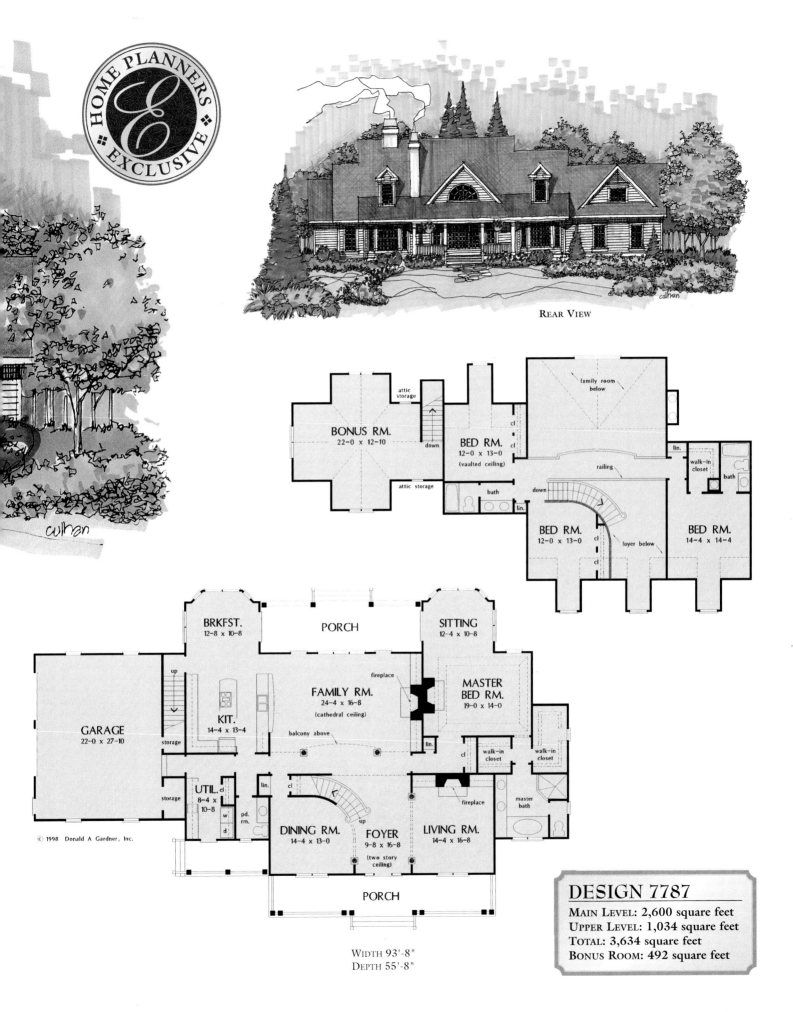

REAR VIEW

attic storage

down

BONUS RM.
22-0 x 12-10

attic storage

BED RM.
12-0 x 13-0
(vaulted ceiling)

family room
below

cl

cl

lin.

walk-in
closet

bath

bath

lin.

railing

down

foyer below

BED RM.
12-0 x 13-0

cl

cl

cl

BED RM.
14-4 x 14-4

BRKFST.
12-8 x 10-8

PORCH

SITTING
12-4 x 10-8

up

KIT.
14-4 x 13-4

fireplace

FAMILY RM.
24-4 x 16-8
(cathedral ceiling)

balcony above

storage

MASTER
BED RM.
19-0 x 14-0

lin.

cl

walk-in
closet

walk-in
closet

GARAGE
22-0 x 27-10

storage

UTIL.
8-4 x
10-8

cl

lin.

cl

master
bath

fireplace

w

d

pd.
rm.

DINING RM.
14-4 x 13-0

FOYER
9-8 x 16-8
(two story
ceiling)

up

LIVING RM.
14-4 x 16-8

© 1998 Donald A Gardner, Inc.

PORCH

WIDTH 93'-8"
DEPTH 55'-8"

DESIGN 7787

MAIN LEVEL: 2,600 square feet
UPPER LEVEL: 1,034 square feet
TOTAL: 3,634 square feet
BONUS ROOM: 492 square feet

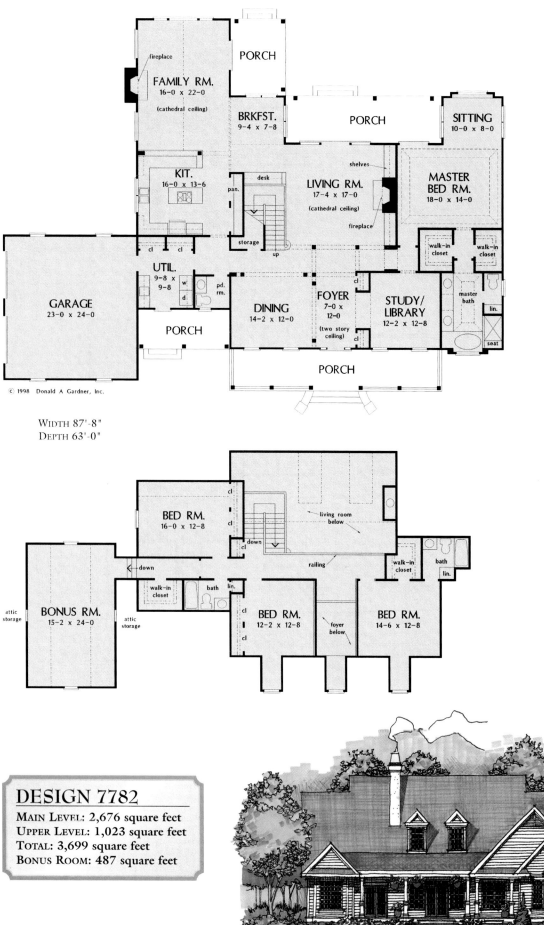

PORCH

FAMILY RM.
16-0 x 22-0
(cathedral ceiling)

fireplace

PORCH

BRKFST.
9-4 x 7-8

SITTING
10-0 x 8-0

KIT.
16-0 x 13-6

desk

pan.

shelves

LIVING RM.
17-4 x 17-0
(cathedral ceiling)

fireplace

MASTER
BED RM.
18-0 x 14-0

storage

up

walk-in
closet

walk-in
closet

cl

cl

UTIL.
9-8 x
9-8

w.

d.

pd.
rm.

cl

master
bath

lin.

GARAGE
23-0 x 24-0

DINING
14-2 x 12-0

FOYER
7-0 x
12-0
(two story
ceiling)

STUDY/
LIBRARY
12-2 x 12-8

seat

cl

PORCH

PORCH

© 1998 Donald A Gardner, Inc.

WIDTH 87'-8"
DEPTH 63'-0"

BED RM.
16-0 x 12-8

cl

cl

cl

living room
below

down

down

railing

walk-in
closet

bath

lin.

BONUS RM.
15-2 x 24-0

attic
storage

attic
storage

walk-in
closet

bath

lin.

cl

BED RM.
12-2 x 12-8

foyer
below

BED RM.
14-6 x 12-8

cl

DESIGN 7782

MAIN LEVEL: 2,676 square feet
UPPER LEVEL: 1,023 square feet
TOTAL: 3,699 square feet
BONUS ROOM: 487 square feet

REAR VIEW

THE *Rutledge*

*Balusters and columns and a wide front porch
create a country-style exterior reminiscent of soft
summer evenings spent watching fireflies and
sipping sun tea. Indeed, an aura of hospitality
prevails throughout this well-planned design.*

Teeming with luxury and style, this gracious country estate features spacious rooms, volume ceilings and four porches for extended outdoor living. Fireplaces in the living and family rooms grant warmth and character to these spacious gathering areas, while columns add definition to the open living and dining rooms. Built-in bookshelves in the living room are both attractive and func-tional, as is the built-in desk adjacent to the open, U-shaped staircase. The main suite is more haven than bedroom with a tray ceiling, sitting alcove, dual walk-ins and luxury bath. The upstairs balcony overlooks both foyer and living room while serving as an open, central hallway for the home's three family bedrooms and bonus room.

Art for Crafts Sake

Dreamy bungalows and Craftsman-style homes

© 1999 Donald A. Gardner, Inc.

THE *Amber Ridge*

A quaint covered porch suggests comfortable living in this attractive design. Cedar shakes, shutters and gables add to the Craftsman-style character of the facade.

A number of desirable exterior and interior elements combine to create this attractive Arts and Crafts style home. Stone, siding and cedar shakes enhance the home's facade, while its interior boasts an open floor plan for a feeling of spaciousness and a split-bedroom design for homeowner privacy. A cathedral ceiling caps the great room with a central fireplace and flanking built-in cabinets. With a center island stovetop, the kitchen is spacious and efficiently designed. The main suite is positioned for privacy and features a bay window, tray ceiling, dual walk-in closets and a deluxe private bath. Two more family bedrooms are located on the first floor, and a fourth can be found on the lower level along with a sizable recreation room. This home is designed with a walk-out basement.

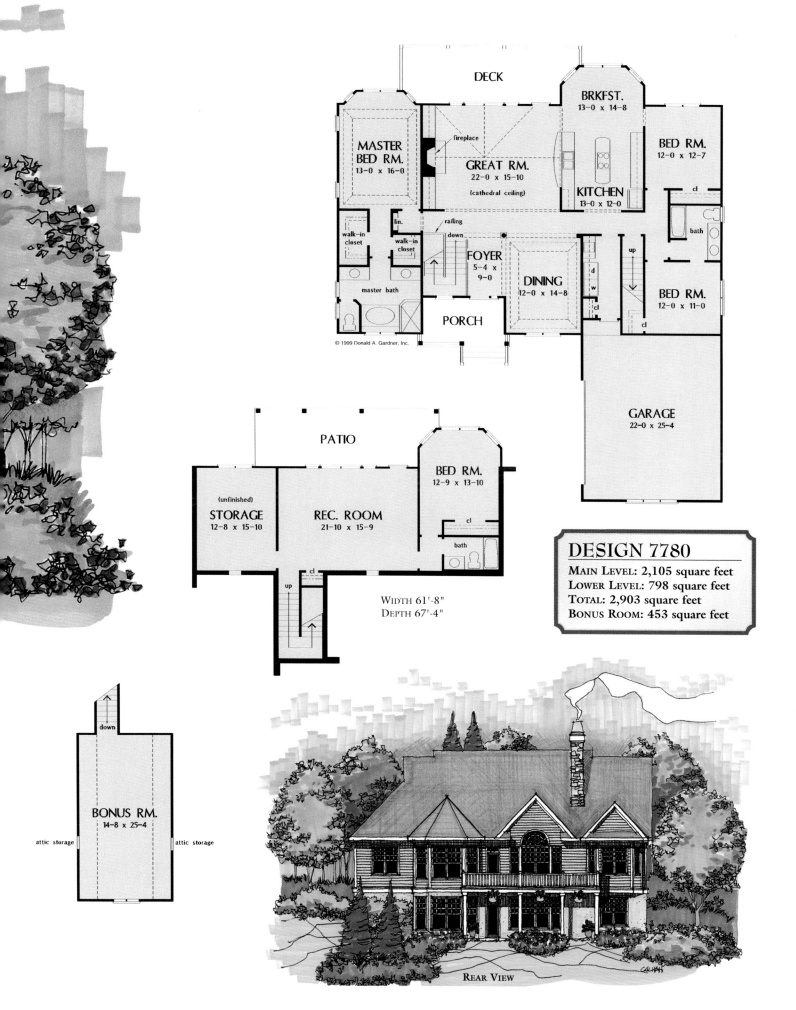

DECK

MASTER
BED RM.
13-0 x 16-0

fireplace

GREAT RM.
22-0 x 15-10

(cathedral ceiling)

BRKFST.
13-0 x 14-8

BED RM.
12-0 x 12-7

KITCHEN
13-0 x 12-0

cl

bath

walk-in
closet

lin.

walk-in
closet

railing

down

FOYER
5-4 x
9-0

DINING
12-0 x 14-8

up

d

w

cl

BED RM.
12-0 x 11-0

master bath

PORCH

cl

© 1999 Donald A. Gardner, Inc.

GARAGE
22-0 x 25-4

PATIO

BED RM.
12-9 x 13-10

(unfinished)
STORAGE
12-8 x 15-10

REC. ROOM
21-10 x 15-9

cl

bath

cl

up

WIDTH 61'-8"
DEPTH 67'-4"

DESIGN 7780

MAIN LEVEL: 2,105 square feet
LOWER LEVEL: 798 square feet
TOTAL: 2,903 square feet
BONUS ROOM: 453 square feet

down

BONUS RM.
14-8 x 25-4

attic storage

attic storage

REAR VIEW

Dreamy bungalows and Craftsman-style homes **117**

© 1999 Donald A. Gardner, Inc.

THE *Saxony*

*Cedar shakes, stucco and window detailing all combine to
give this home plenty of Craftsman-style character. The
time period could be the early 20th Century, when the
Arts and Crafts Movement was at its peak.*

Multiple gables, cedar shakes, stucco and stone provide plenty of enchantment for the exterior of this hillside home. Craftsman character abounds inside as well as out, evidenced by the home's functional floor plan. Built-ins flank the great rooms's fireplace for convenience, and a rear deck extends living space outdoors. The exceptionally well-designed kitchen features an island stovetop and an adjacent breakfast bay. The main suite, also with a bay window, enjoys two walk-in closets and a delightful bath with dual vanities. Two upstairs bedrooms are divided by an impressive balcony overlooking both the foyer and great room. A fourth bedroom and generous recreation room are located on the lower level, while a spacious bonus room provides more room for expansion above the garage. This home is designed with a walk-out basement.

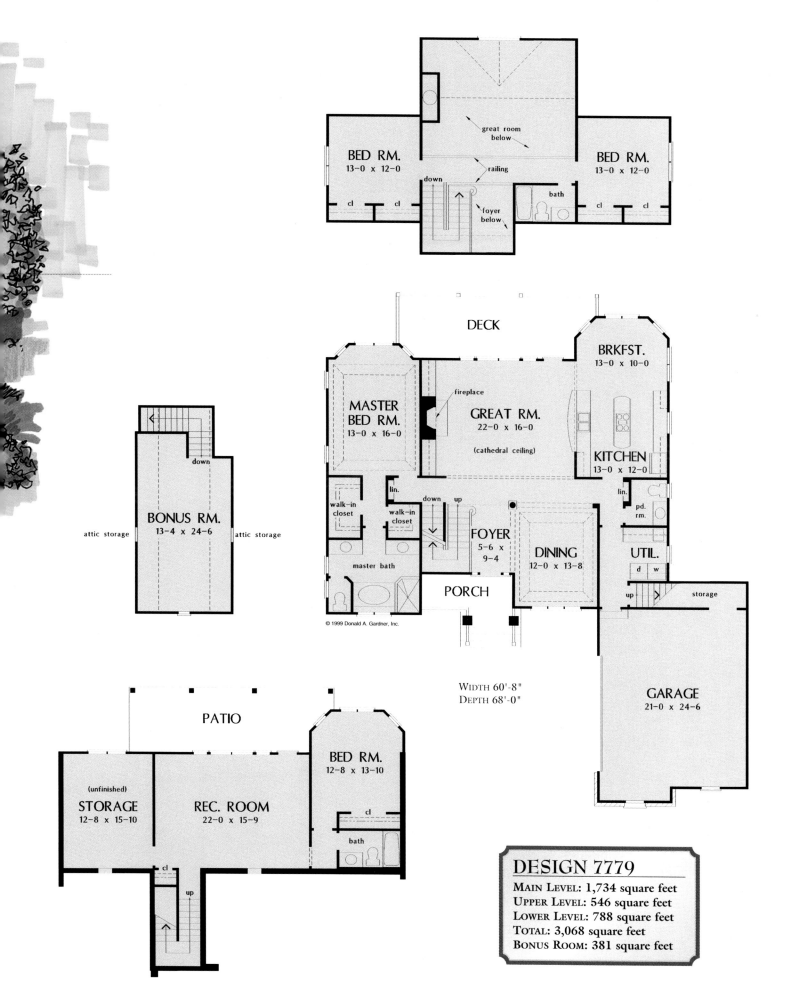

BED RM.
13-0 x 12-0

great room
below

railing

down

foyer
below

bath

BED RM.
13-0 x 12-0

cl   cl

cl   cl

BONUS RM.
13-4 x 24-6

down

attic storage   attic storage

DECK

BRKFST.
13-0 x 10-0

MASTER
BED RM.
13-0 x 16-0

fireplace

GREAT RM.
22-0 x 16-0

(cathedral ceiling)

KITCHEN
13-0 x 12-0

lin.

lin.

pd.
rm.

walk-in
closet

walk-in
closet

down   up

master bath

FOYER
5-6 x
9-4

DINING
12-0 x 13-8

UTIL.

d w

up

storage

PORCH

© 1999 Donald A. Gardner, Inc.

WIDTH 60'-8"
DEPTH 68'-0"

GARAGE
21-0 x 24-6

PATIO

BED RM.
12-8 x 13-10

STORAGE
(unfinished)
12-8 x 15-10

REC. ROOM
22-0 x 15-9

cl

bath

cl

up

DESIGN 7779
MAIN LEVEL: 1,734 square feet
UPPER LEVEL: 546 square feet
LOWER LEVEL: 788 square feet
TOTAL: 3,068 square feet
BONUS ROOM: 381 square feet

Dreamy bungalows and Craftsman-style homes 119

*F*orm and function blend wonderfully together in this Arts and Crafts style home. A bold combination of exterior building materials elicits interest outside, while inside, a practical design creates space in the home's economical floor plan. To maximize space, the foyer, great room, dining room and kitchen are completely open to one another. A cathedral ceiling spans the great room and kitchen, expanding the rooms vertically. The bedrooms are split for ultimate main suite privacy, and a cathedral ceiling caps the main bedroom for an added sense of space. A bonus room, accessed near the main suite, offers options for storage and expansion. Two family bedrooms and a hall bath are located on the opposite side of the home.

DESIGN 7790
SQUARE FOOTAGE: 1,437
BONUS ROOM: 297 square feet

WIDTH 53'-4"
DEPTH 49'-8"

© 1998 Donald A Gardner, Inc.

THE *Tanglewood*

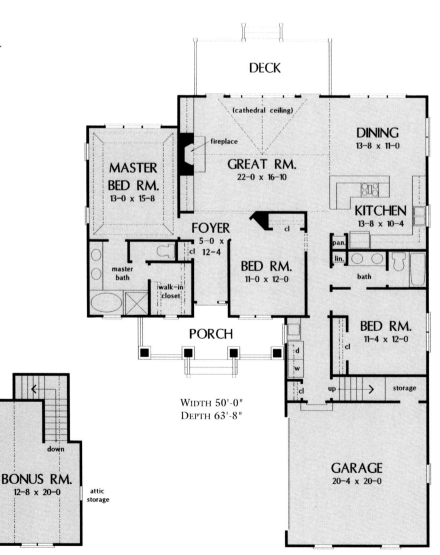

THE *Lochmere*

Stucco, stone and cedar shakes create an interesting exterior for this attractive three-bedroom bungalow. A cathedral ceiling with a rear clerestory dormer embellishes the generous great room, creating additional space and appeal. The dining room and efficiently designed kitchen are open to one another and to the great room for casual, relaxed living. The main suite features an elegant tray ceiling and a private bath with an enclosed toilet and walk-in closet. A bonus room over the garage allows for ample storage and future expansion.

DESIGN 7793

SQUARE FOOTAGE: 1,700
BONUS ROOM: 294 square feet

DECK

(cathedral ceiling)

fireplace

MASTER BED RM.
13-0 x 15-8

GREAT RM.
22-0 x 16-10

DINING
13-8 x 11-0

KITCHEN
13-8 x 10-4

FOYER
5-0 x 12-4

cl

cl

pan.

lin.

master bath

walk-in closet

BED RM.
11-0 x 12-0

bath

BED RM.
11-4 x 12-0

cl

PORCH

d

w

cl

up

storage

WIDTH 50'-0"
DEPTH 63'-8"

GARAGE
20-4 x 20-0

BONUS RM.
12-8 x 20-0

down

attic storage

attic storage

© 1998 Donald A. Gardner, Inc.

© 1998 Donald A. Gardner, Inc.

© 1999 Donald A. Gardner, Inc.

THE *Ravencroft*

Craftsman was the dominant style for small homes built after the turn of the century until the early 1920s. This design is a modern interpretation of the style with such typical details as stick-work, wood shakes, pillars defining a covered porch, Craftsman window detail and a stone-and-siding facade.

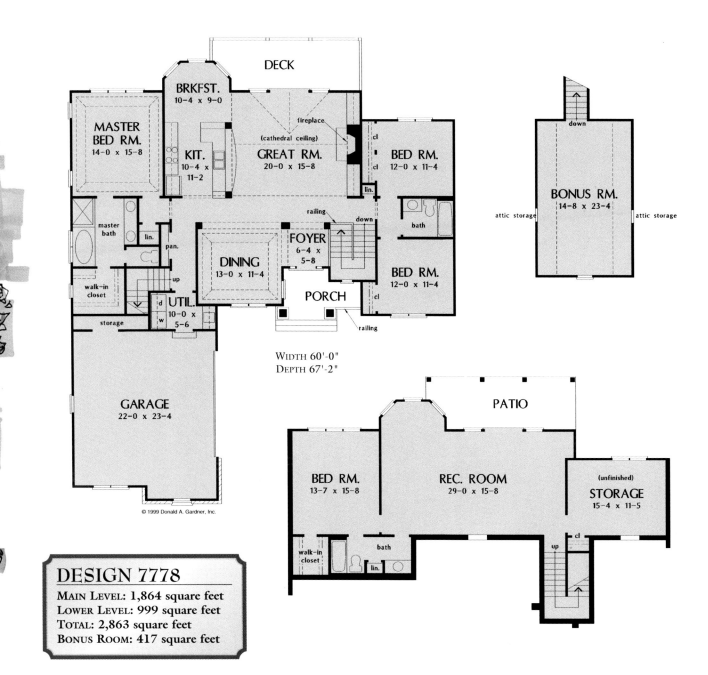

DECK

BRKFST.
10-4 x 9-0

MASTER
BED RM.
14-0 x 15-8

KIT.
10-4 x
11-2

GREAT RM.
20-0 x 15-8

fireplace

(cathedral ceiling)

BED RM.
12-0 x 11-4

cl
cl

lin.

bath

master
bath

lin.

pan.

railing

down

FOYER
6-4 x
5-8

DINING
13-0 x 11-4

BED RM.
12-0 x 11-4

walk-in
closet

up

storage

UTIL.
10-0 x
5-6

d
w

PORCH

cl

railing

GARAGE
22-0 x 23-4

WIDTH 60'-0"
DEPTH 67'-2"

© 1999 Donald A. Gardner, Inc.

down

BONUS RM.
14-8 x 23-4

attic storage

attic storage

PATIO

BED RM.
13-7 x 15-8

REC. ROOM
29-0 x 15-8

(unfinished)
STORAGE
15-4 x 11-5

walk-in
closet

bath

lin.

cl

up

DESIGN 7778

MAIN LEVEL: 1,864 square feet
LOWER LEVEL: 999 square feet
TOTAL: 2,863 square feet
BONUS ROOM: 417 square feet

REAR VIEW

*C*edar shakes, siding and stone blend art-
fully together on the exterior of this
attractive Craftsman-style home. Inside, a
remarkably open floor plan separates the main
suite from two family bedrooms for homeowner
privacy. Optimizing family togetherness, the
common areas of the home are surprisingly open
with few interior walls to divide the rooms from
one another. A tray ceiling adds definition to the
dining room, while the great room is amplified
by a cathedral ceiling. A tray ceiling also tops the
main bedroom, which enjoys a lovely, private
bath with a walk-in closet. Two family bedrooms
share a hall bath on the opposite side of the
home, and another bedroom is located downstairs along with a large recreation room and
unfinished storage area. This home is designed
with a walk-out basement.

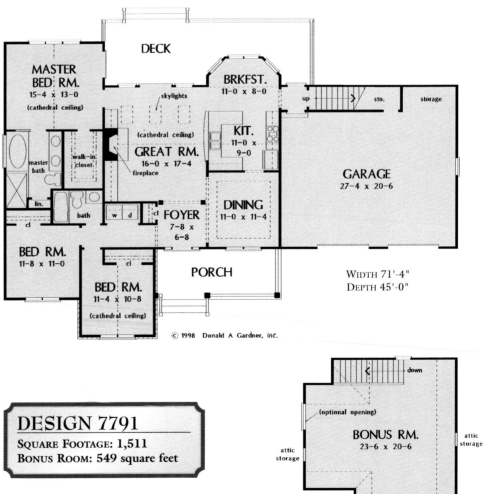

© 1998 Donald A. Gardner, Inc.

THE *Windemere*

A smart mixture of exterior building materials, striking gables and Craftsman character creates this impressive home's warm, welcoming facade. Located at the heart of the home is a great room that possesses a number of outstanding features, including a cathedral ceiling, fireplace, convenient built-ins, a trio of skylights and access to the rear deck. The main bedroom also enjoys deck entry as well as a cathedral ceiling, walk-in closet and private bath with a linen closet and roomy shower. Two more bedrooms share a hall bath at the front of the home. The oversized garage allows for ample storage, while a large bonus room above can fulfill many needs.

DECK

MASTER BED RM.
15-4 x 13-0
(cathedral ceiling)

BRKFST.
11-0 x 8-0

skylights

master bath

walk-in closet

(cathedral ceiling)

KIT.
11-0 x 9-0

up

sto.

storage

GREAT RM.
16-0 x 17-4
fireplace

lin.

bath

cl

w   d

cl

FOYER
7-8 x 6-8

DINING
11-0 x 11-4

GARAGE
27-4 x 20-6

BED RM.
11-8 x 11-0

cl

BED RM.
11-4 x 10-8
(cathedral ceiling)

PORCH

WIDTH 71'-4"
DEPTH 45'-0"

© 1998 Donald A Gardner, Inc.

DESIGN 7791
SQUARE FOOTAGE: 1,511
BONUS ROOM: 549 square feet

down

(optional opening)

attic storage

BONUS RM.
23-6 x 20-6

attic storage

*B*old front-facing gables, arched windows and a mixture of stone, stucco and cedar shakes create an interesting exterior for this Craftsman-style home. Inside, the floor plan is open and casual with few walls dividing the common areas of the home. A cathedral ceiling enhances the great room, while a rear deck and a screened porch expand living space to the outdoors. The main bedroom is topped by a tray ceiling and features deck access, linen and walk-in closets and an exquisite private bath. Two family bedrooms, one with a cathedral ceiling, and a hall bath are located nearby.

DECK

SCREEN PORCH
9-4 x 13-0

DINING
12-0 x 13-4

GREAT RM.
17-0 x 21-0
(cathedral ceiling)

fireplace

MASTER BED RM.
17-4 x 13-4

walk-in closet

lin.

bath

master bath

BRKFST.
10-0 x 10-0

pan.

KIT.
12-0 x 12-4

FOYER
9-8 x 6-4

cl

cl

lin.

BED RM.
11-0 x 12-0

cl

w d

UTIL.
9-8 x 5-8

PORCH

BED RM.
11-0 x 12-0
(cathedral ceiling)

WIDTH 66'-2"
DEPTH 58'-6"

GARAGE
22-0 x 22-0

storage

Ⓒ 1998 Donald A Gardner, Inc.

DESIGN 7792
SQUARE FOOTAGE: 1,933

THE *Kidwell*

© 1998 Donald A. Gardner, Inc.

culhen

Dreamy bungalows and Craftsman-style homes **125**

© 1998 Donald A. Gardner, Inc.

THE *Serenade*

Stone, stucco and cedar shakes combine to create an enchanting exterior for this split-bedroom, Craftsman bungalow. A tray ceiling adds elegance and definition to the open dining room, while the great room is enhanced by a cathedral ceiling and fireplace with flanking built-ins. The spacious, efficiently designed kitchen features a useful center island and is open to both the breakfast bay and great room. The main suite enjoys a bay window, tray ceiling, dual walk-in closets and private bath. Two family bedrooms share a hall bath on the opposite side of the home near access to a versatile bonus room.

DECK

BRKFST.
13-0 x 10-0

(cathedral ceiling)

MASTER BED RM.
13-0 x 18-0

fireplace

GREAT RM.
22-0 x 16-0

KITCHEN
13-0 x 12-0

BED RM./STUDY
12-0 x 12-4

shelves

bath

walk-in closet

walk-in closet

cl

UTIL.
6-0 x 12-8

up

master bath

pd. rm.

FOYER
6-6 x 9-8

DINING
12-0 x 14-8

BED RM.
12-0 x 12-4

PORCH

© 1998 Donald A. Gardner, Inc.

WIDTH 61'-8"
DEPTH 69'-9"

GARAGE
22-0 x 25-4

storage

down

BONUS RM.
14-8 x 25-4

attic storage

attic storage

DESIGN 7795
SQUARE FOOTAGE: 2,152
BONUS ROOM: 453 square feet

© 1998 Donald A. Gardner, Inc.

THE *Caledon*

DESIGN 7794

MAIN LEVEL: 1,734 square feet
UPPER LEVEL: 547 square feet
TOTAL: 2,281 square feet
BONUS ROOM: 381 square feet

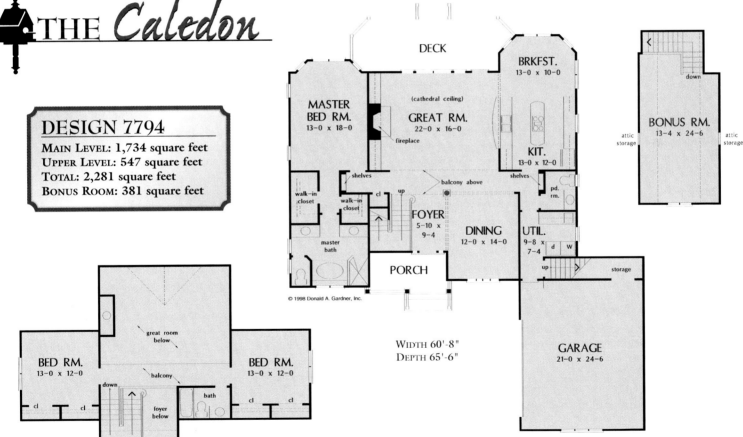

DECK

BRKFST.
13-0 x 10-0

MASTER BED RM.
13-0 x 18-0

GREAT RM.
22-0 x 16-0
(cathedral ceiling)
fireplace

KIT.
13-0 x 12-0

shelves

walk-in closet

walk-in closet

balcony above

up

cl

FOYER
5-10 x 9-4

DINING
12-0 x 14-0

UTIL.
9-8 x 7-4

pd. rm.

shelves

master bath

PORCH

up

storage

d w

© 1998 Donald A. Gardner, Inc.

WIDTH 60'-8"
DEPTH 65'-6"

GARAGE
21-0 x 24-6

BONUS RM.
13-4 x 24-6
attic storage
attic storage
down

BED RM.
13-0 x 12-0

great room below

balcony

BED RM.
13-0 x 12-0

down

foyer below

bath

cl

Siding, stone and a trio of front-facing gables add character to the facade of this captivating cottage with courtyard garage. The second-floor balcony overlooks a two-story foyer and the great room with a cathedral ceiling. An open and undefined central hall on the first floor is bordered on either end by built-in arch niches. Bay windows extend both the breakfast area and main bedroom. The main suite features dual walk-in closets and a private bath with twin vanities, separate tub and shower and enclosed toilet. Divided by the upstairs balcony are two family bedrooms. Accessed from the first floor, a bonus room offers options for future expansion.

THE *Heathridge*

Among the most distinctive features of the Craftsman style are the places where the roof joins the wall. Typically, the rafter edges are exposed and often extra stick-work is added, as shown here.

© 1998 Donald A. Gardner, Inc.

REAR VIEW

DECK

BED RM.
15-0 x 14-8

cl

bath

lin.

pd. rm.

w d

UTILITY
10-0 x 8-0

cl

BRKFST.
13-4 x 10-2

KITCHEN
13-4 x 11-4

pan.

DINING
13-4 x 12-0

GREAT RM.
19-0 x 19-4

fireplace

(cathedral ceiling)

railing   down

FOYER
7-8 x
9-2

cl

PORCH

MASTER
BED RM.
15-0 x 17-0

walk-in
closet

walk-in
closet

lin.   master bath

WIDTH 72'-4"
DEPTH 66'-0"

© 1998 Donald A. Gardner, Inc.

GARAGE
21-0 x 23-2

storage

DESIGN 7776

MAIN LEVEL: 2,068 square feet
UPPER LEVEL: 930 square feet
TOTAL: 2,998 square feet

PATIO

UNFIN. STORAGE/
MECHANICAL
28-4 x 18-8

FAMILY RM.
19-0 x 18-6

fireplace

BED RM.
14-6 x 15-0

lin.   cl

bath

up

*T*his Craftsman-style home takes advantage of hillside views with its deck, patio and abundance of rear windows. An open floor plan enhances the home's spaciousness. The great room features a cathedral ceiling, access to the generous rear deck and a fireplace with built-in cabinets and shelves. Designed for ultimate efficiency, the kitchen serves the great room, dining room and breakfast area with equal ease. A tray ceiling lends elegance to the main bedroom, which features deck access and two walk-in closets. An extravagant bath boasts dual vanities, a large linen closet and a separate tub and shower. A second main bedroom is located on the opposite side of the house. Downstairs, a spacious family room with fireplace, a third bedroom and full bath complete the plan. This home is designed with a walk-out basement.

THE *Vandenberg*

*Exposed rafter beams, distinctive pillars, vintage
windows and a cross-gabled roof all combine to give
this design the warm feeling of a Craftsman-style
home—a style as popular today as it was
in the early decades of the 20th Century.*

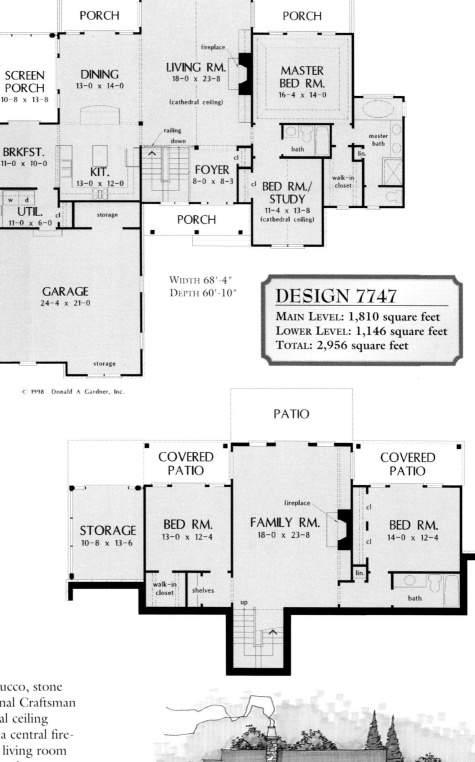

PORCH

PORCH

SCREEN
PORCH
10-8 x 13-8

DINING
13-0 x 14-0

LIVING RM.
18-0 x 23-8

fireplace

MASTER
BED RM.
16-4 x 14-0

(cathedral ceiling)

master
bath

BRKFST.
11-0 x 10-0

KIT.
13-0 x 12-0

railing
down

bath

FOYER
8-0 x 8-3

cl

lin.

walk-in
closet

w   d

UTIL.
11-0 x 6-0

cl

storage

PORCH

cl

BED RM./
STUDY
11-4 x 13-8
(cathedral ceiling)

GARAGE
24-4 x 21-0

WIDTH 68'-4"
DEPTH 60'-10"

storage

DESIGN 7747

MAIN LEVEL: 1,810 square feet
LOWER LEVEL: 1,146 square feet
TOTAL: 2,956 square feet

(c) 1998 Donald A Gardner, Inc.

PATIO

COVERED
PATIO

COVERED
PATIO

STORAGE
10-8 x 13-6

BED RM.
13-0 x 12-4

fireplace

FAMILY RM.
18-0 x 23-8

cl

cl

BED RM.
14-0 x 12-4

walk-in
closet

shelves

up

lin.

bath

This hillside home combines stucco, stone and cedar shakes for exceptional Craftsman character. A dramatic cathedral ceiling heightens the open living room with a central fireplace and built-ins. Porches flank the living room to allow uninterrupted views of the outdoors through its rear wall of windows. The two rear porches are entered through the dining room and main bedroom, while the breakfast and dining rooms enjoy screened porch access. The main bedroom is topped by a tray ceiling and features a lovely private bath and walk-in closet. A versatile bedroom/study and full bath are nearby. Downstairs are two more bedrooms, each with an adjacent covered patio, another full bath and a generous family room with fireplace. This home is designed with a walk-out basement.

REAR VIEW

THE *Peekskill*

A good choice for cold climates, the steep pitch of the cross-gabled roof will stop snow build-up cold! Attractive wood panels march across triple garage doors, capped by twin dormers bringing light into an enormous bonus room.

A stunning center dormer with an arched window embellishes the exterior of this Craftsman-style home with a walkout basement. The dormer's arched window allows light into the foyer, which boasts a built-in niche. The second floor's hall is a balcony that overlooks both foyer and great room. A generous back porch extends the great room, which features an impressive vaulted ceiling and fireplace, while a tray ceiling adorns the formal dining room. The main bedroom, which has a tray ceiling as well, enjoys back porch access, a built-in cabinet, a generous walk-in closet and private bath. Two more bedrooms are located upstairs, while a fourth can be found in the basement along with a family room. Note the huge bonus room over the three-car garage.

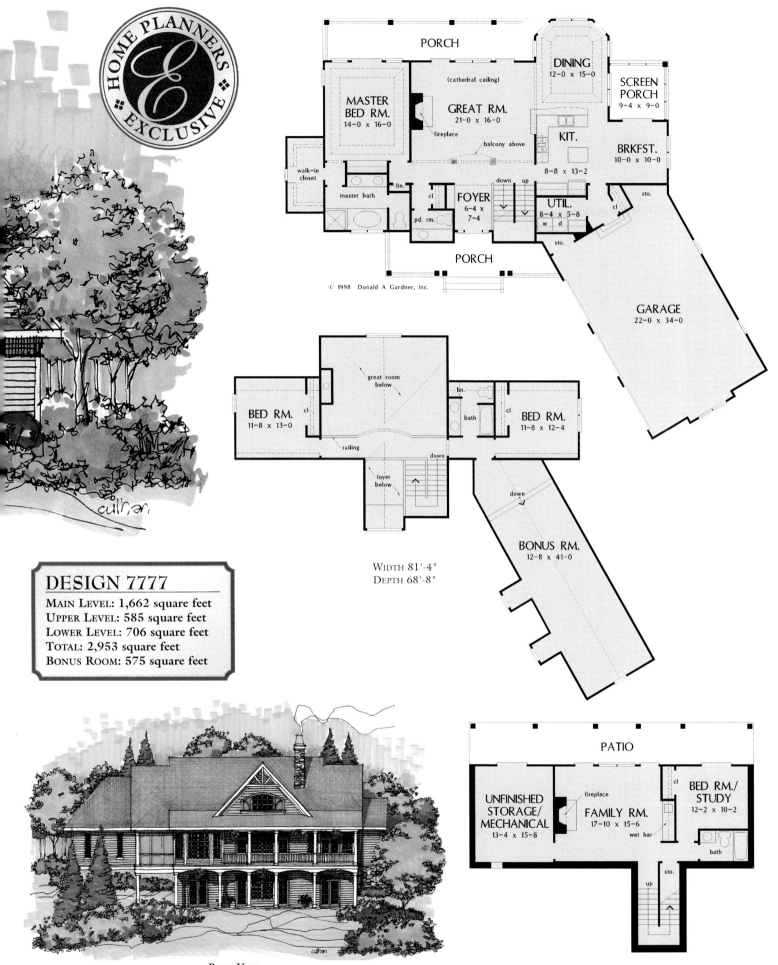

PORCH

DINING
12-0 x 15-0

SCREEN PORCH
9-4 x 9-0

MASTER BED RM.
14-0 x 16-0

GREAT RM.
21-0 x 16-0

(cathedral ceiling)

fireplace

balcony above

KIT.
8-8 x 13-2

BRKFST.
10-0 x 10-0

walk-in closet

master bath

lin.

cl

FOYER
6-4 x 7-4

down   up

UTIL.
8-4 x 5-8

w   d

sto.

pd. rm.

cl

sto.

PORCH

© 1998 Donald A Gardner, Inc.

GARAGE
22-0 x 34-0

great room below

lin.

bath

cl

BED RM.
11-8 x 13-0

cl

BED RM.
11-8 x 12-4

railing

down

foyer below

down

BONUS RM.
12-8 x 41-0

WIDTH 81'-4"
DEPTH 68'-8"

DESIGN 7777

MAIN LEVEL: 1,662 square feet
UPPER LEVEL: 585 square feet
LOWER LEVEL: 706 square feet
TOTAL: 2,953 square feet
BONUS ROOM: 575 square feet

PATIO

UNFINISHED STORAGE/ MECHANICAL
13-4 x 15-8

fireplace

FAMILY RM.
17-10 x 15-6

wet bar

cl

BED RM./ STUDY
12-2 x 10-2

bath

sto.

up

REAR VIEW

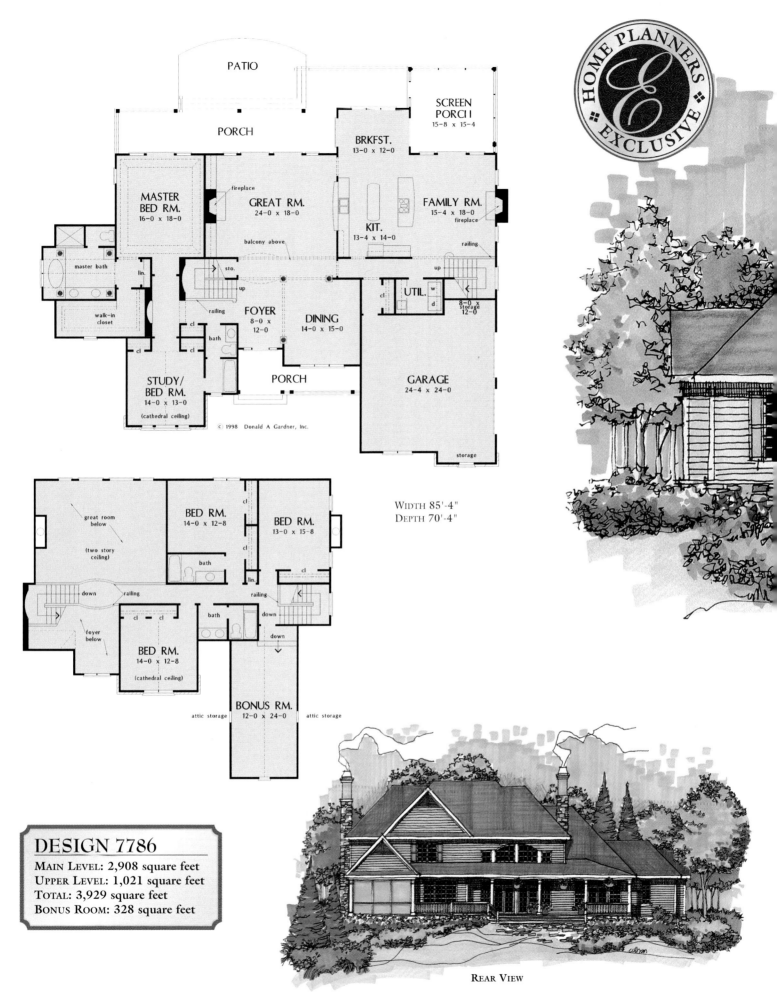

PATIO

PORCH

SCREEN PORCH
15-8 x 15-4

BRKFST.
13-0 x 12-0

fireplace

MASTER BED RM.
16-0 x 18-0

GREAT RM.
24-0 x 18-0

FAMILY RM.
15-4 x 18-0
fireplace

KIT.
13-4 x 14-0

master bath

balcony above

railing

up

walk-in closet

lin.

sto.

up

UTIL.
w
d

cl

8-0 x storage
12-0

railing

FOYER
8-0 x 12-0

DINING
14-0 x 15-0

cl

bath

cl

STUDY/ BED RM.
14-0 x 13-0
(cathedral ceiling)

PORCH

GARAGE
24-4 x 24-0

© 1998 Donald A Gardner, Inc.

storage

great room below

(two story ceiling)

BED RM.
14-0 x 12-8

cl

cl

BED RM.
13-0 x 15-8

cl

bath

lin.

down

railing

railing

down

foyer below

cl — cl

bath

down

BED RM.
14-0 x 12-8
(cathedral ceiling)

attic storage

BONUS RM.
12-0 x 24-0

attic storage

WIDTH 85'-4"
DEPTH 70'-4"

REAR VIEW

DESIGN 7786
MAIN LEVEL: 2,908 square feet
UPPER LEVEL: 1,021 square feet
TOTAL: 3,929 square feet
BONUS ROOM: 328 square feet

HOME PLANNERS EXCLUSIVE

THE *Knightsbridge*

*This fine estate is embellished with such wonderful
details as multi-pane windows capped by circular
accent lights. Inspired by Craftsman-style design, a
blend of rustic and contemporary elements are
drawn together by a simple theme.*

Siding and stone embellish the exterior of this five-bed-
room traditional estate for an exciting, yet stately,
appearance. A two-story foyer creates an impressive
entry for this nearly 4,000 square foot home. An equally
impressive two-story great room features a fireplace, built-ins
and back-porch access. The island kitchen is open and generous, centrally located to conveniently service the great room,
family room, dining room, breakfast area and back porches.
The first-floor main suite enjoys an elegant tray ceiling, back-
porch access and a lavish bath with all the amenities. A
study/bedroom with cathedral ceiling and adjacent bath are
also located on the first floor. Three bedrooms, two baths and
a bonus room can be found upstairs.

© 1999 Donald A. Gardner, Inc.

THE *Chesapeake*

The covered porch is marked by special stick-work and double pilasters. The theme of Craftsman styling captures the heart with its varying roofline, rafter details and stone-and-siding exterior.

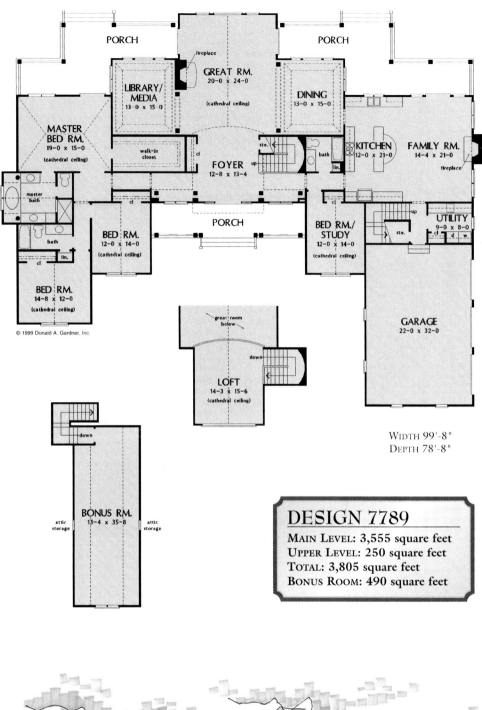

PORCH

PORCH

GREAT RM.
20-0 x 24-0
(cathedral ceiling)

fireplace

LIBRARY/
MEDIA
13-0 x 15-0

DINING
13-0 x 15-0

MASTER
BED RM.
19-0 x 15-0
(cathedral ceiling)

walk-in
closet

cl

KITCHEN
12-0 x 21-0

FAMILY RM.
14-4 x 21-0

fireplace

sto.

bath

up

lin.

FOYER
12-8 x 13-4

master
bath

bath

cl

cl

BED RM.
12-0 x 14-0
(cathedral ceiling)

PORCH

BED RM./
STUDY
12-0 x 14-0
(cathedral ceiling)

sto.

up

UTILITY
9-0 x 8-0

cl

lin.

BED RM.
14-8 x 12-0
(cathedral ceiling)

© 1999 Donald A. Gardner, Inc.

GARAGE
22-0 x 32-0

great room
below

LOFT
14-3 x 15-6
(cathedral ceiling)

down

WIDTH 99'-8"
DEPTH 78'-8"

down

BONUS RM.
13-4 x 35-8

attic
storage

attic
storage

DESIGN 7789

MAIN LEVEL: 3,555 square feet
UPPER LEVEL: 250 square feet
TOTAL: 3,805 square feet
BONUS ROOM: 490 square feet

This extraordinary four-bedroom estate features multiple gables with decorative wood brackets, arched windows and a stone and siding facade for undeniable Craftsman character. At the heart of the home, a magnificent cathedral ceiling adds space and stature to the impressive great room, which accesses both back porches. Sharing the great room's cathedral ceiling, the loft makes an excellent reading nook. Tray ceilings adorn the dining room and library/media room, while all four bedrooms enjoy cathedral ceilings. A sizable kitchen opens to a large gathering room for ultimate family togetherness. The main suite features back-porch access, a lavish, private bath and an oversized walk-in closet. A spacious bonus room is located over the three-car garage for further expansion.

REAR VIEW

THE *Berkshire*

Prominent twin gables and an arched clerestory window lend a custom touch to the rustic facade of this stunning home. A glass-paneled entry announces the bright foyer, which opens to a well-planned interior.

© 1998 Donald A. Gardner, Inc.

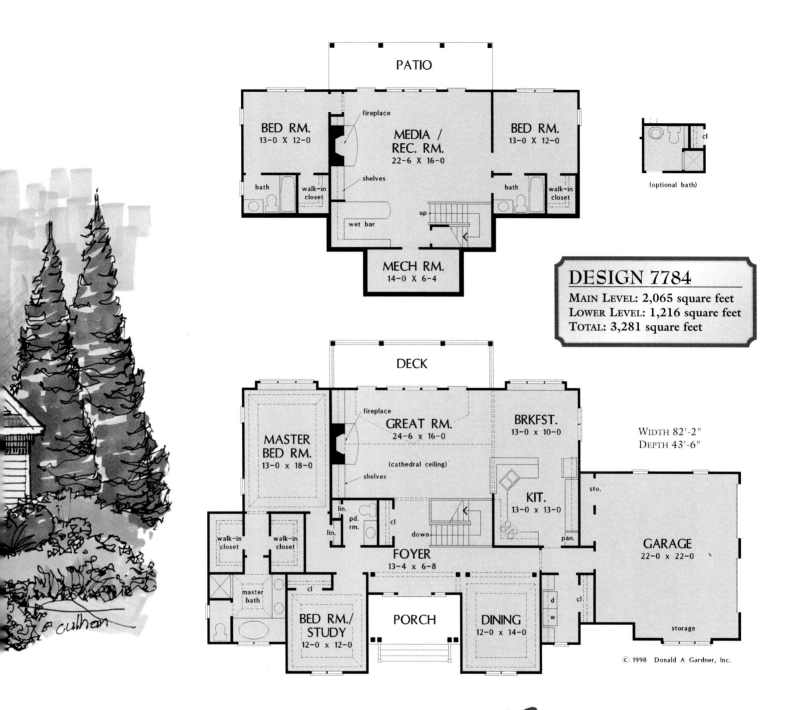

PATIO

BED RM.
13-0 X 12-0

MEDIA /
REC. RM.
22-6 X 16-0

BED RM.
13-0 X 12-0

fireplace

shelves

bath

walk-in
closet

bath

walk-in
closet

wet bar

up

(optional bath)

cl

MECH RM.
14-0 X 6-4

DESIGN 7784

MAIN LEVEL: 2,065 square feet
LOWER LEVEL: 1,216 square feet
TOTAL: 3,281 square feet

DECK

MASTER
BED RM.
13-0 x 18-0

fireplace

GREAT RM.
24-6 x 16-0

(cathedral ceiling)

shelves

BRKFST.
13-0 x 10-0

WIDTH 82'-2"
DEPTH 43'-6"

walk-in
closet

walk-in
closet

lin.

pd.
rm.

cl

lin.

KIT.
13-0 x 13-0

sto.

down

master
bath

cl

FOYER
13-4 x 6-8

pan.

GARAGE
22-0 x 22-0

BED RM./
STUDY
12-0 x 12-0

PORCH

DINING
12-0 x 14-0

d

w

cl

storage

© 1998   Donald A Gardner, Inc.

REAR VIEW

*S*tone, siding and multiple gables combine beautifully on the exterior of this hillside home with a walk-out basement. Taking advantage of rear views, the home's most oft used rooms are oriented at the back with plenty of windows. Augmented by a cathedral ceiling, the great room features a fireplace, built-in shelves and access to the rear deck. Twin walk-in closets and a private bath infuse the main suite with luxury. The nearby powder room offers an optional full bath arrangement allowing the study to double as a bedroom. Downstairs, a large media/recreation room with a wet bar and fireplace separates two more bedrooms, each with a full bath and walk-in closet.

THE *Crowne Canyon*

Almost too grand to be called a garage, this great estate provides enough space for three vehicles plus! Natural light illuminates the interior through attractive transom windows and overhead dormers.

A stunning center dormer with arched window and decorative wood brackets caps the entry to this extraordinary hillside estate. Exposed wood beams enhance the magnificent cathedral ceilings of the foyer, great room, dining room, main bedroom and screened porch, while ten-foot ceilings top the remainder of the first floor. The great room takes in scenic rear views through a wall of windows shared by the media/recreation room. Fireplaces add warmth and ambience to the great room, media/recreation room, screened porch and the main suite's sitting room /study. The kitchen is complete with its center island cooktop, pantry and ample room for two or more cooks. A three-and-a-half car garage allows space for storage or a golf cart. This home is designed with a walk-out basement.

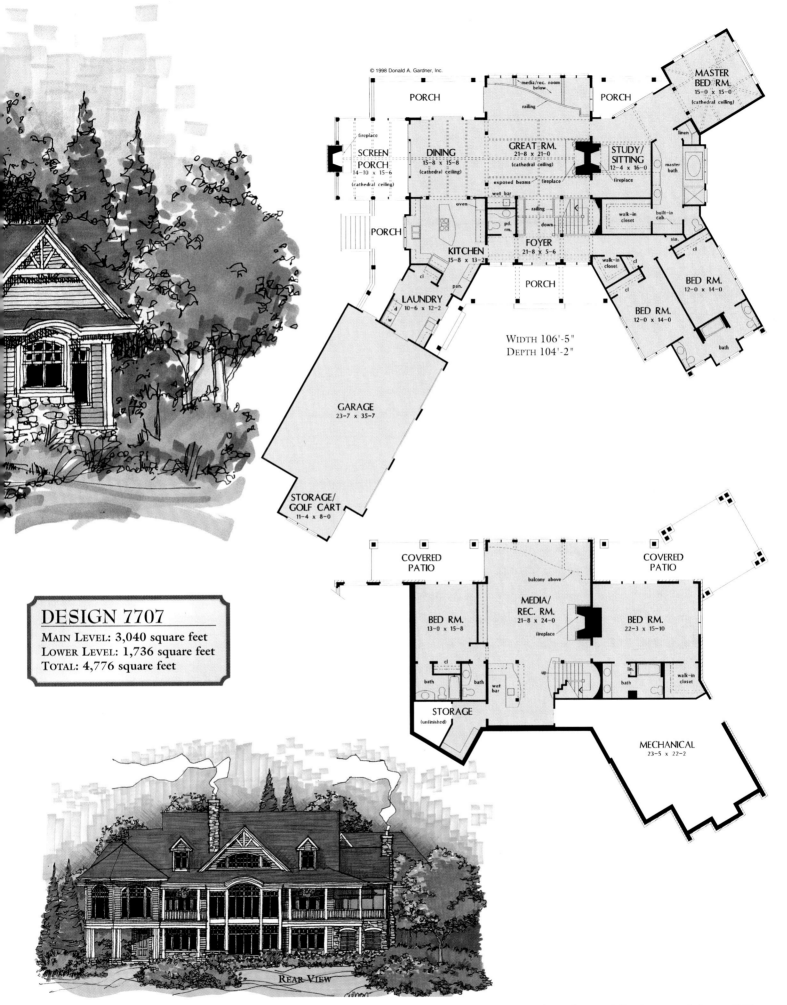

© 1998 Donald A. Gardner, Inc.

PORCH

media/rec. room below

railing

PORCH

MASTER BED RM.
15-0 x 15-0
(cathedral ceiling)

fireplace

SCREEN PORCH
14-10 x 15-6
(cathedral ceiling)

DINING
15-8 x 15-8
(cathedral ceiling)

GREAT RM.
21-8 x 21-0
(cathedral ceiling)

STUDY/SITTING
12-4 x 16-0
fireplace

linen

master bath

exposed beams

fireplace

wet bar

oven

PORCH

pd. rm.

railing

down

walk-in closet

built-in cab.

sto.

cl

KITCHEN
15-8 x 13-2

FOYER
21-8 x 5-6

walk-in closet

cl

cl

BED RM.
12-0 x 14-0

cl

pan.

PORCH

LAUNDRY
10-6 x 12-2

d

w

BED RM.
12-0 x 14-0

bath

WIDTH 106'-5"
DEPTH 104'-2"

GARAGE
23-7 x 35-7

STORAGE/GOLF CART
11-4 x 8-0

COVERED PATIO

balcony above

COVERED PATIO

BED RM.
13-0 x 15-8

MEDIA/REC. RM.
21-8 x 24-0
fireplace

BED RM.
22-3 x 15-10

cl

bath

bath

wet bar

up

lin.

bath

walk-in closet

STORAGE
(unfinished)

MECHANICAL
23-5 x 22-2

DESIGN 7707

MAIN LEVEL: 3,040 square feet
LOWER LEVEL: 1,736 square feet
Total: 4,776 square feet

REAR VIEW

Dreamy bungalows and Craftsman-style homes 141

THE *Amherst*

Classic styling extends to the garage's facade. Elements such as Craftsman-style windows, a stone-and-siding exterior and rafter details all combine to mark this impressive home with the special charm of the Arts and Crafts era.

Dormers, gables with wood brackets, a double-door entry and a stone and siding exterior lend charm and sophistication to this Craftsman estate. Cathedral ceilings and fireplaces are standard in the living room, family room and main bedroom, while the living room, family room and study feature built-in bookshelves. The spacious kitchen with island stovetop and walk-in pantry opens completely to the family room and breakfast area. The main suite excels with a private sitting room, access to its own porch, two oversized walk-in closets and a lavish bath. Overlooking both foyer and living room, the second floor balcony connects two bedrooms, a library and a bonus room.

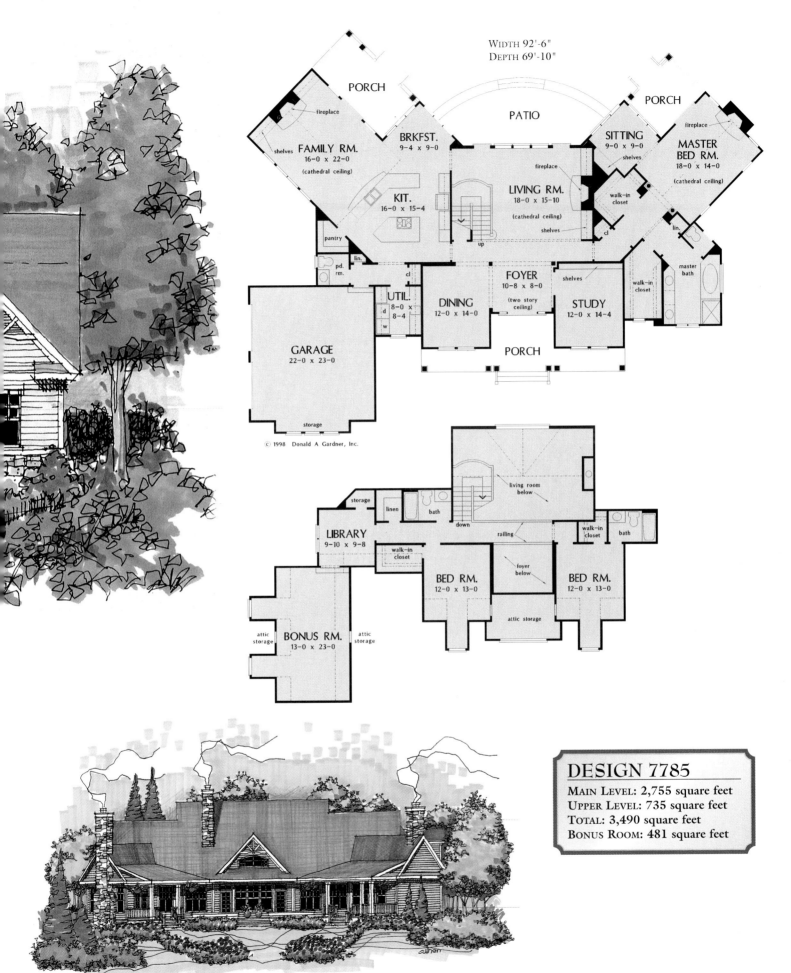

WIDTH 92'-6"
DEPTH 69'-10"

PORCH

PORCH

PATIO

FAMILY RM.
16-0 x 22-0
(cathedral ceiling)

fireplace

shelves

BRKFST.
9-4 x 9-0

SITTING
9-0 x 9-0

shelves

MASTER
BED RM.
18-0 x 14-0
(cathedral ceiling)

fireplace

KIT.
16-0 x 15-4

LIVING RM.
18-0 x 15-10
(cathedral ceiling)

fireplace

walk-in
closet

pantry

shelves

cl

lin.

lin.

pd.
rm.

cl

up

master
bath

walk-in
closet

UTIL.
8-0 x
8-4

DINING
12-0 x 14-0

FOYER
10-8 x 8-0
(two story
ceiling)

shelves

STUDY
12-0 x 14-4

walk-in
closet

d

w

GARAGE
22-0 x 23-0

PORCH

storage

© 1998   Donald A Gardner, Inc.

storage

living room
below

linen

bath

LIBRARY
9-10 x 9-8

down

railing

walk-in
closet

bath

walk-in
closet

BED RM.
12-0 x 13-0

foyer
below

BED RM.
12-0 x 13-0

attic storage

attic
storage

BONUS RM.
13-0 x 23-0

attic
storage

DESIGN 7785

MAIN LEVEL: 2,755 square feet
UPPER LEVEL: 735 square feet
TOTAL: 3,490 square feet
BONUS ROOM: 481 square feet

REAR VIEW

THE *Esperance*

With a kind of country version of Craftsman styling,
this dreamy bungalow is sure to be a real winner.
A metal porch roof combined with traditional
Craftsman elements only enhance this home's appeal.

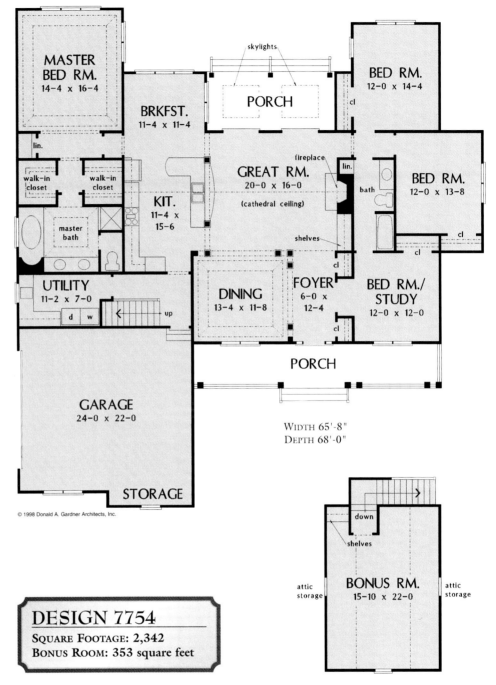

MASTER BED RM.
14-4 x 16-4

BRKFST.
11-4 x 11-4

skylights

PORCH

BED RM.
12-0 x 14-4

cl

lin.

walk-in closet

walk-in closet

KIT.
11-4 x 15-6

fireplace

GREAT RM.
20-0 x 16-0
(cathedral ceiling)

lin.

bath

BED RM.
12-0 x 13-8

master bath

shelves

cl

cl

cl

UTILITY
11-2 x 7-0

d w

up

DINING
13-4 x 11-8

FOYER
6-0 x 12-4

cl

BED RM./
STUDY
12-0 x 12-0

cl

GARAGE
24-0 x 22-0

PORCH

WIDTH 65'-8"
DEPTH 68'-0"

STORAGE

© 1998 Donald A. Gardner Architects, Inc.

down

shelves

attic storage

BONUS RM.
15-10 x 22-0

attic storage

DESIGN 7754
SQUARE FOOTAGE: 2,342
BONUS ROOM: 353 square feet

Stone siding, cedar shakes and a metal porch roof adorn the facade of this irresistible Craftsman-style home. An open floor plan and special ceiling treatments enhance spaciousness in the home's common living areas. The dining room enjoys a graceful tray ceiling and multiple columns, while a shared cathedral ceiling expands the great room and kitchen. A duo of double doors connect the great room to the skylit back porch. The main suite is a homeowner's retreat with a tray ceiling, two walk-in closets, a linen closet and tray-ceilinged bath with dual sink vanity, garden tub, shower and private toilet. Three more bedrooms share a unique hall bath. A large utility room and bonus room complete the plan.

© 1998 Donald A. Gardner, Inc.

THE *Monte Vista*

Graceful stick-work, cedar shakes and a stone-and-siding exterior lend a Craftsman-type air to this fabulous home. A segmental fanlight and sidelights make a classic accent to an impressive entry.

A variety of exterior materials and interesting windows combine with an unusual floor plan to make this an exceptional home. It is designed for a sloping lot, with full living quarters on the main level, but with two extra bedrooms and a family room added to the basement level. A covered porch showcases a wonderful dining-room window and an attractive front door. The living room, enhanced by a fireplace, adjoins the dining room for easy entertaining. The island kitchen and a bayed breakfast room are to the left. Three bedrooms on this level include one that is well placed to serve as a study. The main suite enjoys dual vanities, a garden tub and a walk-in closet. A deck on this floor covers a patio off the lower-level family room, which has its own fireplace. This home is designed with a walk-out basement.

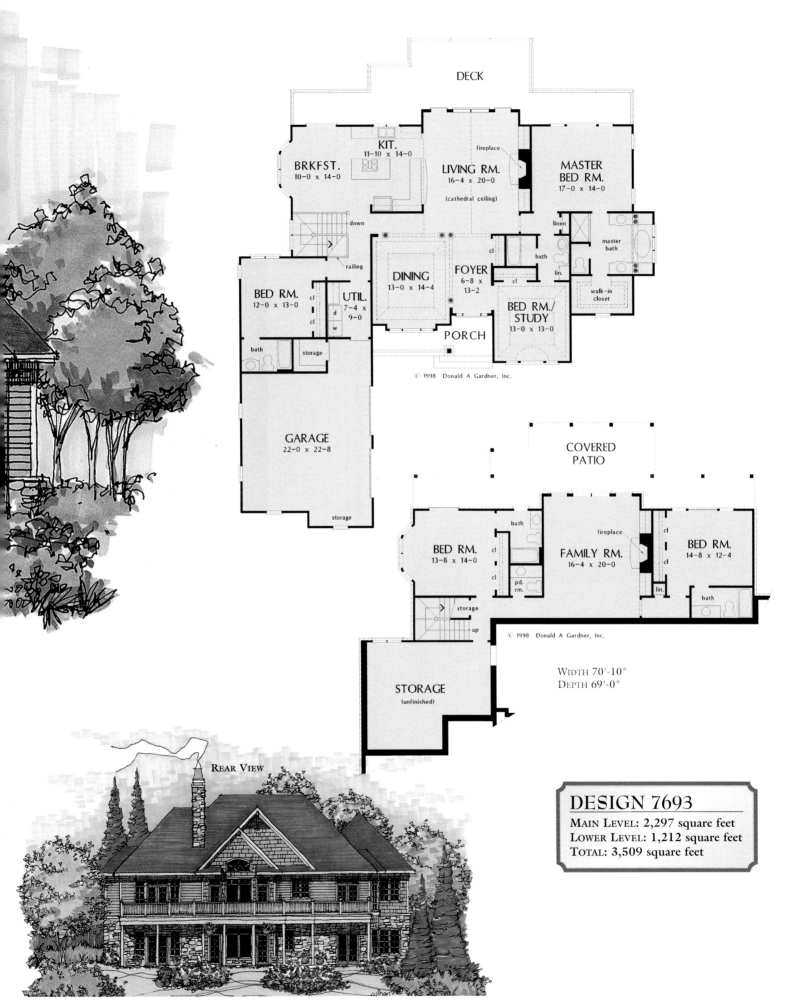

DECK

KIT.
11-10 x 14-0

BRKFST.
10-0 x 14-0

fireplace

LIVING RM.
16-4 x 20-0

(cathedral ceiling)

MASTER
BED RM.
17-0 x 14-0

down

railing

linen

master
bath

lin.

walk-in
closet

cl

bath

BED RM.
12-0 x 13-0

cl

cl

UTIL.
7-4 x
9-0

d

w

DINING
13-0 x 14-4

FOYER
6-8 x
13-2

cl

BED RM./
STUDY
13-0 x 13-0

bath

storage

PORCH

GARAGE
22-0 x 22-8

storage

© 1998 Donald A Gardner, Inc.

COVERED
PATIO

bath

BED RM.
13-8 x 14-0

cl

cl

cl

pd.
rm.

fireplace

FAMILY RM.
16-4 x 20-0

cl

lin.

cl

BED RM.
14-8 x 12-4

bath

storage

up

© 1998 Donald A Gardner, Inc.

STORAGE
(unfinished)

WIDTH 70'-10"
DEPTH 69'-0"

REAR VIEW

DESIGN 7693

MAIN LEVEL: 2,297 square feet
LOWER LEVEL: 1,212 square feet
TOTAL: 3,509 square feet

© 1998 Donald A. Gardner, Inc.

THE *Aurora*

This fabulous design has many charming architectural features that make it a country version of a Craftsman classic. Among the most distinctive features of the style is a wide-eave overhang, which is often decorated with special woodwork.

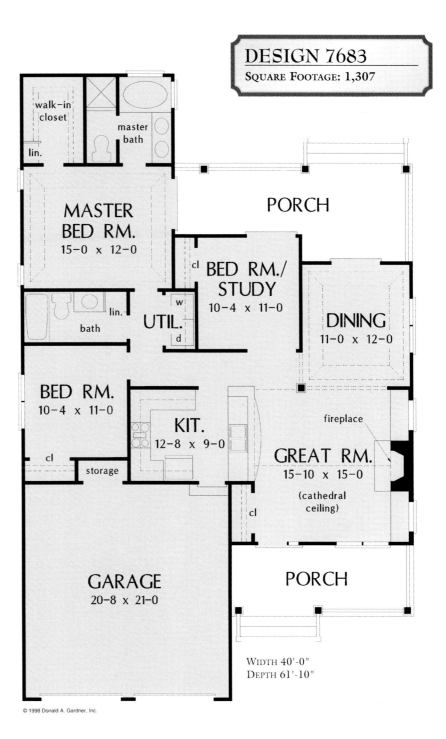

© 1998 Donald A. Gardner, Inc.

DESIGN 7683

SQUARE FOOTAGE: 1,307

walk-in closet

lin.

master bath

MASTER BED RM.
15-0 x 12-0

bath

lin.

UTIL.

cl

BED RM./ STUDY
10-4 x 11-0

PORCH

DINING
11-0 x 12-0

BED RM.
10-4 x 11-0

cl

storage

KIT.
12-8 x 9-0

fireplace

GREAT RM.
15-10 x 15-0

(cathedral ceiling)

cl

GARAGE
20-8 x 21-0

PORCH

WIDTH 40'-0"
DEPTH 61'-10"

Matchstick details highlight the asymmetrical gables of this charming country home. A quaint covered porch leads to a spacious great room with a centered fireplace framed by windows. A formal dining room with a tray ceiling has rear-porch access. The heart of the home is a U-shaped kitchen, which provides a service entrance from the garage. The secluded main suite has a double-bowl lavatory and a walk-in closet with additional linen storage. Two additional bedrooms—or make one a study—share a full bath and a hall laundry.

THE *Avalon*

© 1998 Donald A. Gardner, Inc.

Custom details accent this stone and wood-siding home.
Designed with numerous windows to maximize
exterior views, a special circular window
complements a sunny bumped-out bay.

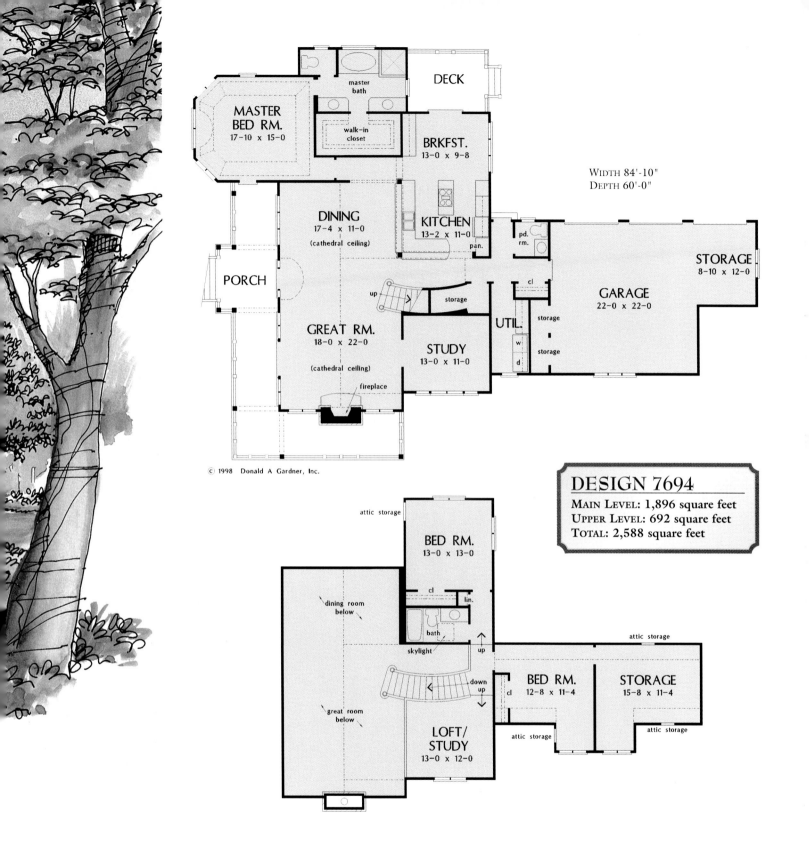

master
bath

DECK

MASTER
BED RM.
17-10 x 15-0

walk-in
closet

BRKFST.
13-0 x 9-8

WIDTH 84'-10"
DEPTH 60'-0"

DINING
17-4 x 11-0
(cathedral ceiling)

KITCHEN
13-2 x 11-0

pan.

pd.
rm.

STORAGE
8-10 x 12-0

PORCH

up

storage

cl

GARAGE
22-0 x 22-0

GREAT RM.
18-0 x 22-0

(cathedral ceiling)

STUDY
13-0 x 11-0

UTIL.

storage

w

d

storage

fireplace

© 1998 Donald A Gardner, Inc.

attic storage

BED RM.
13-0 x 13-0

DESIGN 7694

MAIN LEVEL: 1,896 square feet
UPPER LEVEL: 692 square feet
TOTAL: 2,588 square feet

dining room
below

cl

lin.

bath

skylight

up

attic storage

great room
below

down
up

BED RM.
12-8 x 11-4

STORAGE
15-8 x 11-4

LOFT/
STUDY
13-0 x 12-0

attic storage

cl

attic storage

attic storage

*T*his fine three-bedroom home is full of amenities and will be a family favorite! A covered porch leads into the great room/dining room area. Here, a fireplace reigns at one end, casting its glow throughout the room. A private study is tucked away, perfect for a home office or computer study. The main suite offers a bayed sitting area, large walk-in closet and a pampering bath. With plenty of counter and cabinet space and an adjacent breakfast area, the kitchen will be a favorite gathering place for casual meal times. The upstairs family sleeping zone includes two bedrooms, a full bath, a loft/study area and a huge storage room.

© 1998 Donald A. Gardner, Inc.

THE *Hatteras*

The cedar shake exterior is enhanced by a recessed entry announced by twin sets of pilasters and an elliptical arch. Asymmetrical gables with lovely rafter tails top an elevated porch, perfect for waterfront living.

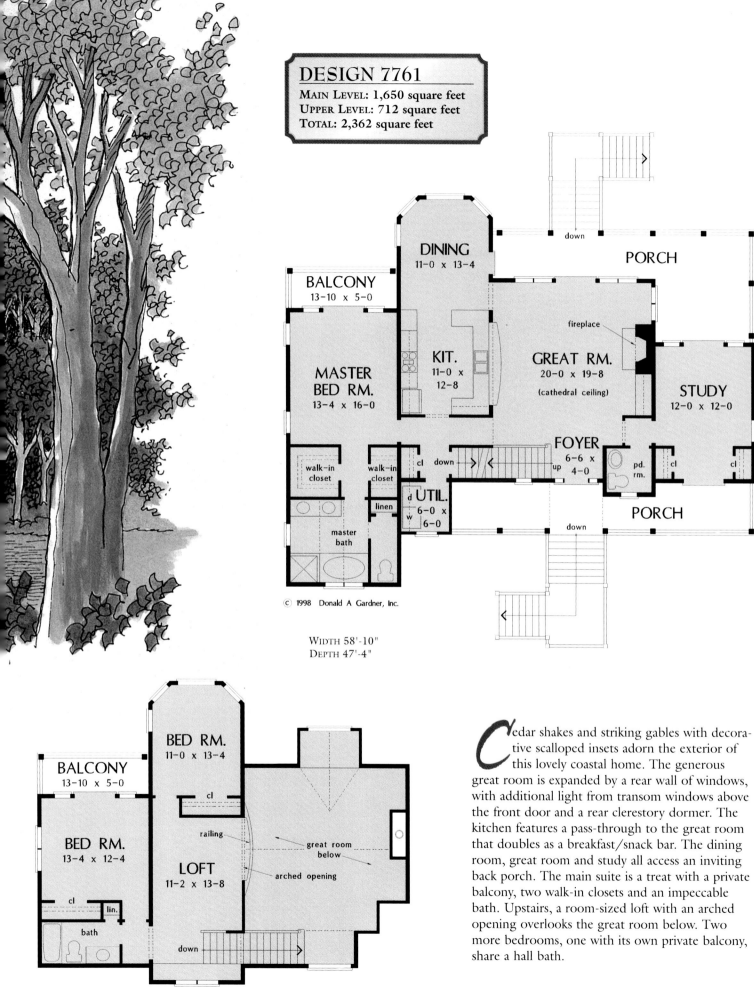

DESIGN 7761

MAIN LEVEL: 1,650 square feet
UPPER LEVEL: 712 square feet
TOTAL: 2,362 square feet

DINING
11-0 x 13-4

PORCH

BALCONY
13-10 x 5-0

KIT.
11-0 x
12-8

fireplace

GREAT RM.
20-0 x 19-8
(cathedral ceiling)

MASTER
BED RM.
13-4 x 16-0

STUDY
12-0 x 12-0

walk-in
closet

walk-in
closet

cl

down

FOYER
6-6 x
4-0

up

pd.
rm.

cl

cl

linen

d UTIL.
6-0 x
6-0

w

master
bath

down

PORCH

down

ⓒ 1998 Donald A Gardner, Inc.

WIDTH 58'-10"
DEPTH 47'-4"

BED RM.
11-0 x 13-4

BALCONY
13-10 x 5-0

cl

railing

great room
below

BED RM.
13-4 x 12-4

LOFT
11-2 x 13-8

arched opening

cl

lin.

bath

down

*C*edar shakes and striking gables with decorative scalloped insets adorn the exterior of this lovely coastal home. The generous great room is expanded by a rear wall of windows, with additional light from transom windows above the front door and a rear clerestory dormer. The kitchen features a pass-through to the great room that doubles as a breakfast/snack bar. The dining room, great room and study all access an inviting back porch. The main suite is a treat with a private balcony, two walk-in closets and an impeccable bath. Upstairs, a room-sized loft with an arched opening overlooks the great room below. Two more bedrooms, one with its own private balcony, share a hall bath.

Heritage Homes

Traditional designs for today's lifestyles

155

THE *Huntington*

Many generously sized, shuttered windows fill this beautiful home with natural light. Traditional styling captures the heart with its multiple gables, sunburst windows and welcoming wide porch.

© 1998 Donald A. Gardner, Inc.

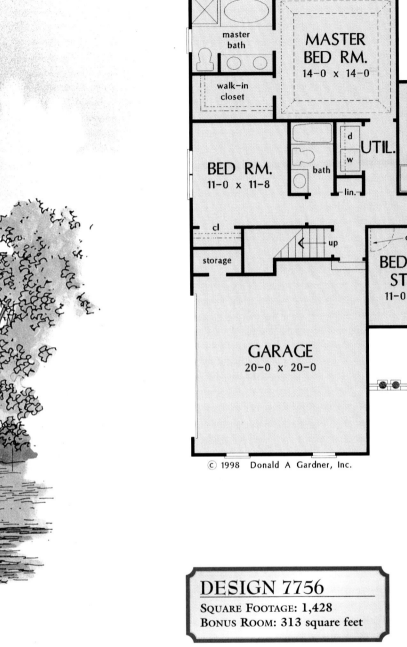

master
bath

walk-in
closet

MASTER
BED RM.
14-0 x 14-0

WIDTH 52'-8"
DEPTH 52'-4"

BED RM.
11-0 x 11-8

UTIL.

bath

d

w

lin.

KIT.
10-0 x
12-8

DINING
11-0 x 12-8

PORCH

cl

storage

up

optional door

BED RM./
STUDY
11-0 x 11-0

cl

cl

fireplace

GREAT RM.
18-0 x 14-8
(cathedral ceiling)

GARAGE
20-0 x 20-0

PORCH

© 1998   Donald A Gardner, Inc.

DESIGN 7756

SQUARE FOOTAGE: 1,428
BONUS ROOM: 313 square feet

down

attic storage

attic storage

BONUS RM.
12-0 x 21-8

S tunning arched windows framed by bold, front-facing gables add to the tremendous curb appeal of this modest home. Topped by a cathedral ceiling and with
porches on either side, the great room is expanded further by its openness to the
dining room and kitchen. Built-ins flank the fireplace for added convenience. Flexibility, so
important in a home this size, is found in the versatile bedroom/study as well as the bonus
room over the garage. The main suite is positioned for privacy at the rear of the home
with a graceful tray ceiling, walk-in closet and private bath. An additional bedroom and a
hall bath complete the plan.

THE *Jackson*

DECK

storage

GARAGE
20-8 x 20-4

DINING
11-0 x 11-2
(cathedral ceiling)

fireplace

GREAT RM.
16-4 x 15-0
(cathedral ceiling)

MASTER BED RM.
12-4 x 15-0
(cathedral ceiling)

walk-in closet

master bath

KIT.
10-8 x 11-6

FOYER
7-8 x 7-8

w d

UTIL.

cl

bath

lin.

© 1995 Donald A. Gardner Architects, Inc.

PORCH

cl

BED RM./STUDY
11-0 x 11-0
(cathedral ceiling)

cl

BED RM.
12-4 x 11-0

WIDTH 69'-0"
DEPTH 39'-0"

A wide-open floor plan puts the emphasis on family living in this modest, single-story home. A cathedral ceiling stretches the length of the plan, stylishly topping the dining room, great room and main bedroom. Cooks will enjoy working in the presentation kitchen that's open to the dining room and great room. The main suite has a walk-in closet and a compartmented bath with a garden tub and twin vanities. One of the two family bedrooms has a cathedral ceiling as well, making it an optional study. A full hall bath and a convenient hallway laundry center complete this plan.

DESIGN 9797
SQUARE FOOTAGE: 1,417

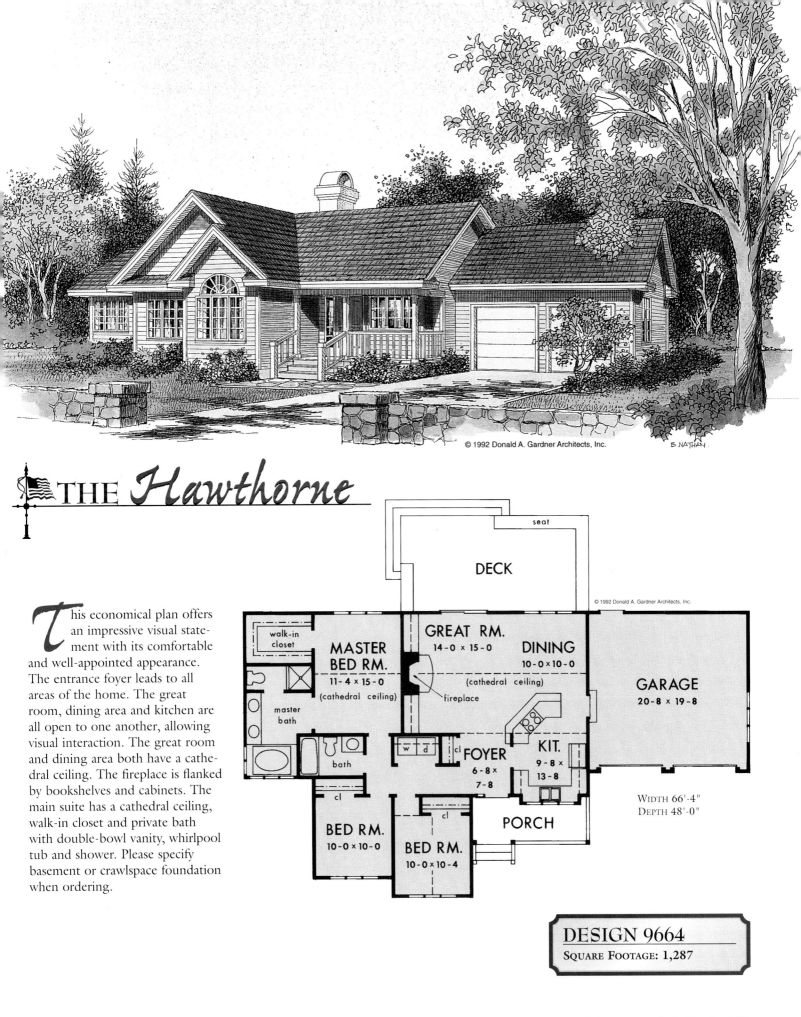

THE *Hawthorne*

This economical plan offers an impressive visual statement with its comfortable and well-appointed appearance. The entrance foyer leads to all areas of the home. The great room, dining area and kitchen are all open to one another, allowing visual interaction. The great room and dining area both have a cathedral ceiling. The fireplace is flanked by bookshelves and cabinets. The main suite has a cathedral ceiling, walk-in closet and private bath with double-bowl vanity, whirlpool tub and shower. Please specify basement or crawlspace foundation when ordering.

© 1992 Donald A. Gardner Architects, Inc.

B. NATHAN

© 1992 Donald A. Gardner Architects, Inc.

DECK
seat

GREAT RM.
14-0 x 15-0

DINING
10-0 x 10-0

(cathedral ceiling)

fireplace

walk-in closet

MASTER BED RM.
11-4 x 15-0
(cathedral ceiling)

master bath

GARAGE
20-8 x 19-8

bath

w d   cl

FOYER
6-8 x 7-8

KIT.
9-8 x 13-8

cl

BED RM.
10-0 x 10-0

cl

BED RM.
10-0 x 10-4

PORCH

WIDTH 66'-4"
DEPTH 48'-0"

DESIGN 9664
SQUARE FOOTAGE: 1,287

A sunny, clerestory dormer in the foyer yields a splendid first impression for this cozy home. The open great room, dining room and kitchen are unified under a shared cathedral ceiling. The adjoining deck provides extra living or entertaining space, while the front bedroom is expanded by a cathedral ceiling that shows off a double window with sunburst accent. The main suite is highlighted by a cathedral ceiling and includes a private bath with garden tub, double-bowl vanity and walk-in closet. A skylit bonus room above the garage offers flexibility and opportunities for growth.

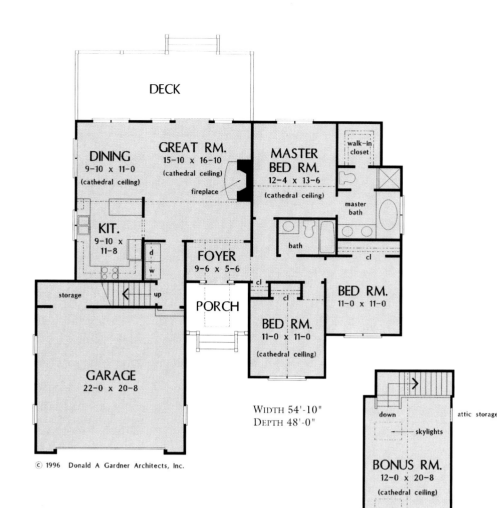

DECK

DINING
9-10 x 11-0
(cathedral ceiling)

GREAT RM.
15-10 x 16-10
(cathedral ceiling)

fireplace

MASTER BED RM.
12-4 x 13-6
(cathedral ceiling)

walk-in closet

master bath

bath

cl

KIT.
9-10 x 11-8

d
w

FOYER
9-6 x 5-6

cl

storage

up

PORCH

cl

BED RM.
11-0 x 11-0

BED RM.
11-0 x 11-0
(cathedral ceiling)

GARAGE
22-0 x 20-8

WIDTH 54'-10"
DEPTH 48'-0"

© 1996 Donald A Gardner Architects, Inc.

down
skylights

attic storage

BONUS RM.
12-0 x 20-8
(cathedral ceiling)

DESIGN 7748
SQUARE FOOTAGE: 1,386
BONUS ROOM: 314 square feet

THE *Oak Grove*

© 1996 Donald A. Gardner Architects, Inc.

B NATHAN

© 1991 Donald A. Gardner Architects, Inc.

R. NATHAN.

THE *Barclay*

DECK

seat

spa

arched window above door

GREAT RM.
15-4 × 18-0
(cathedral ceiling)

fireplace

KIT./BRKFST.
16-8 × 16-0

master bath

walk-in closet

walk-in closet

up

sto.

pd. rm.

cl

MASTER BED RM.
13-0 × 13-6

FOYER
7-8 × 9-0

DINING
12-4 × 12-4

UTILITY
10-0 × 6-4

w
d

PORCH

up

storage

GARAGE
20-0 × 20-0

© 1991 Donald A. Gardner Architects, Inc.

BED RM.
10-4 × 11-9

walk-in closet

down

bath

cl

BED RM.
12-4 × 13-6

down

BONUS RM.
11-0 × 20-0

An arched entrance and windows provide a touch of class to the exterior of this plan. The dining room displays round columns at the entrance while the great room boasts a cathedral ceiling, fireplace and arched window over exterior doors to the deck. The large kitchen is open to the breakfast nook and sliding glass doors present a second access to the deck. In the main suite is a walk-in closet and lavish bath. On the second level are two bedrooms and a full bath. Please specify basement or crawlspace foundation when ordering.

REAR VIEW

DESIGN 9661

MAIN LEVEL: 1,416 square feet
UPPER LEVEL: 445 square feet
TOTAL: 1,861 square feet
BONUS ROOM: 284 square feet

WIDTH 58'-3"
DEPTH 68'-9"

*A*large, center front gable and a covered porch set the tone for a down-home country welcome. The formal dining room is filled with light from a bay window and has direct access to an efficient island kitchen. A matching bay window is found in the breakfast room, furnishing the perfect location for a leisurely cup of morning tea. Active families will enjoy the large great room graced with a warming fireplace and an abundance of windows. For extra flexibility, living space extends out to the covered porch from the great room. An L-shaped staircase leads to the second floor, which contains two family bedrooms, a full bath and a main suite full of amenities. A bonus room extending over the garage can be developed into a game room, fourth bedroom, study or home office at a later date.

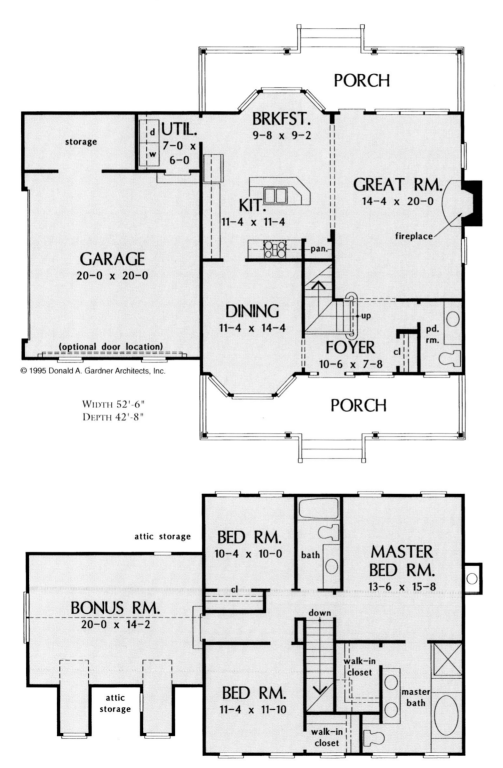

PORCH

UTIL.
7-0 x
6-0

storage

BRKFST.
9-8 x 9-2

GREAT RM.
14-4 x 20-0

fireplace

KIT.
11-4 x 11-4

GARAGE
20-0 x 20-0

pan.

up

DINING
11-4 x 14-4

pd. rm.

cl

FOYER
10-6 x 7-8

(optional door location)

© 1995 Donald A. Gardner Architects, Inc.

PORCH

WIDTH 52'-6"
DEPTH 42'-8"

attic storage

BED RM.
10-4 x 10-0

bath

MASTER
BED RM.
13-6 x 15-8

BONUS RM.
20-0 x 14-2

cl

down

walk-in closet

master bath

attic
storage

BED RM.
11-4 x 11-10

walk-in closet

DESIGN 7600
MAIN LEVEL: 959 square feet
UPPER LEVEL: 833 square feet
TOTAL: 1,792 square feet
BONUS ROOM: 344 square feet

B. NATHAN

THE *Reidville*

Multiple shuttered windows march across the front of this country farmhouse to flood the upper floor with warm, natural light. Delightful dormer windows above the garage illuminate the bonus room, which provides much-needed extra storage space.

© 1998 Donald A. Gardner, Inc.

B. NATHAN

THE *Regency*

Here's a new country home with a fresh face and more than a dash of traditional styling. Classic details include a Palladian window with a keystone accent, which is repeated in miniature above the garage.

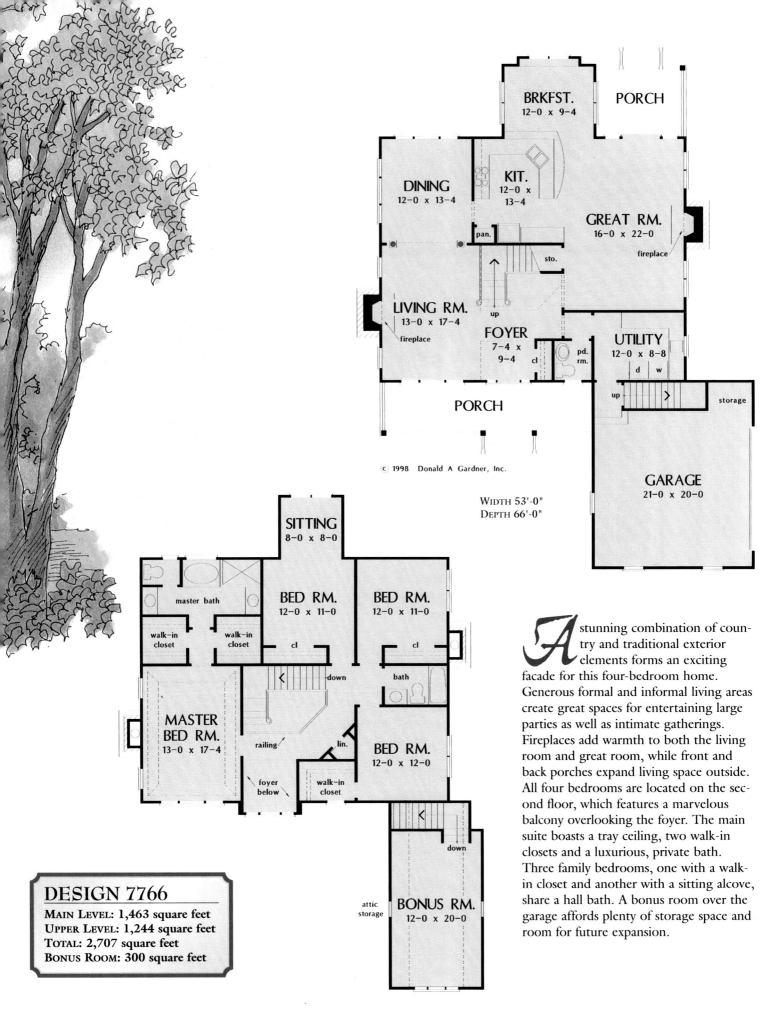

BRKFST.
12-0 x 9-4

PORCH

DINING
12-0 x 13-4

KIT.
12-0 x
13-4

GREAT RM.
16-0 x 22-0

fireplace

pan.

sto.

LIVING RM.
13-0 x 17-4

fireplace

up

FOYER
7-4 x
9-4

cl

pd.
rm.

UTILITY
12-0 x 8-8

d   w

up

storage

PORCH

© 1998   Donald A Gardner, Inc.

WIDTH 53'-0"
DEPTH 66'-0"

GARAGE
21-0 x 20-0

SITTING
8-0 x 8-0

master bath

walk-in
closet

walk-in
closet

BED RM.
12-0 x 11-0

cl

BED RM.
12-0 x 11-0

cl

bath

MASTER
BED RM.
13-0 x 17-4

down

railing

lin.

BED RM.
12-0 x 12-0

foyer
below

walk-in
closet

down

attic
storage

BONUS RM.
12-0 x 20-0

DESIGN 7766

MAIN LEVEL: 1,463 square feet
UPPER LEVEL: 1,244 square feet
TOTAL: 2,707 square feet
BONUS ROOM: 300 square feet

A stunning combination of country and traditional exterior elements forms an exciting facade for this four-bedroom home. Generous formal and informal living areas create great spaces for entertaining large parties as well as intimate gatherings. Fireplaces add warmth to both the living room and great room, while front and back porches expand living space outside. All four bedrooms are located on the second floor, which features a marvelous balcony overlooking the foyer. The main suite boasts a tray ceiling, two walk-in closets and a luxurious, private bath. Three family bedrooms, one with a walk-in closet and another with a sitting alcove, share a hall bath. A bonus room over the garage affords plenty of storage space and room for future expansion.

THE *Springdale*

A varying roofline enhances the facade of this rural retreat. Multi-paned windows with shutters add country character to a home that boasts an open, sophisticated interior design.

© 1995 Donald A. Gardner Architects, Inc.

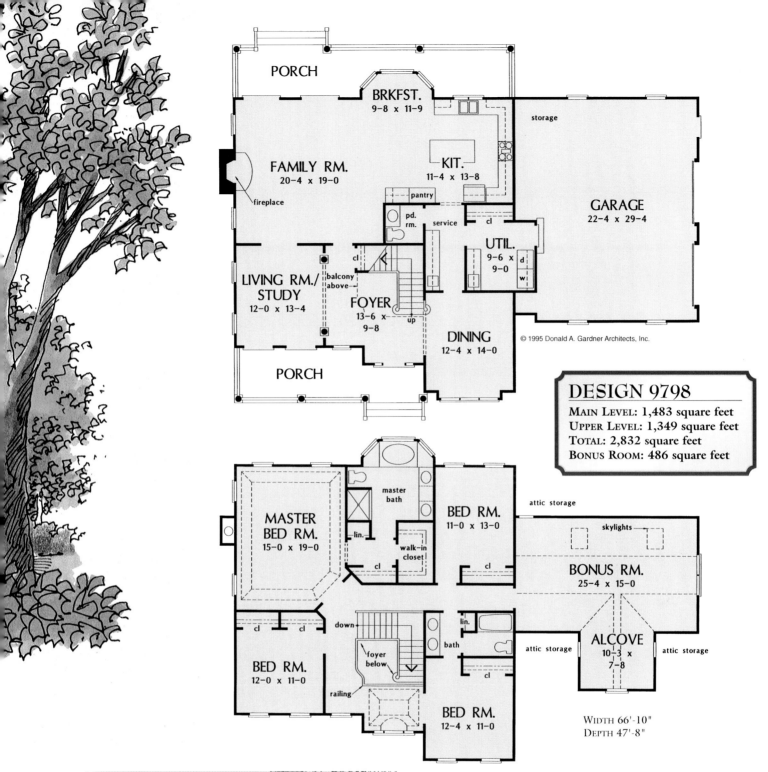

PORCH

BRKFST.
9-8 x 11-9

storage

FAMILY RM.
20-4 x 19-0

fireplace

KIT.
11-4 x 13-8

GARAGE
22-4 x 29-4

pantry

pd. rm.

service

cl

LIVING RM./
STUDY
12-0 x 13-4

balcony above

cl

FOYER
13-6 x 9-8

up

UTIL.
9-6 x 9-0

d w

PORCH

DINING
12-4 x 14-0

© 1995 Donald A. Gardner Architects, Inc.

DESIGN 9798

Main Level: 1,483 square feet
Upper Level: 1,349 square feet
Total: 2,832 square feet
Bonus Room: 486 square feet

master bath

MASTER BED RM.
15-0 x 19-0

lin.

BED RM.
11-0 x 13-0

attic storage

skylights

walk-in closet

cl

cl

BONUS RM.
25-4 x 15-0

cl

cl

down

foyer below

lin.

bath

railing

BED RM.
12-0 x 11-0

cl

ALCOVE
10-3 x 7-8

attic storage

attic storage

BED RM.
12-4 x 11-0

WIDTH 66'-10"
DEPTH 47'-8"

REAR VIEW

*T*his country home displays a quaint rural character outside and a savvy sophistication within. The foyer opens on either side to elegant formal areas, beautifully lit with natural light from multi-pane windows. A casual living area opens to the U-shaped kitchen and bayed breakfast nook and features a focal-point fireplace. The second-floor main suite offers a sumptuous bath with a bumped-out whirlpool tub, twin vanities and a generous walk-in closet. Three family bedrooms share a gallery hall that leads to a spacious bonus room.

THE *Longworth*

Keystone arches, asymmetrical gables and a stunning stucco and stone exterior lend European sophistication to this great design. It presents an Old World look that offers a sense of gracious hospitality as well as stylish comfort.

© 1994 Donald A. Gardner Architects, Inc.

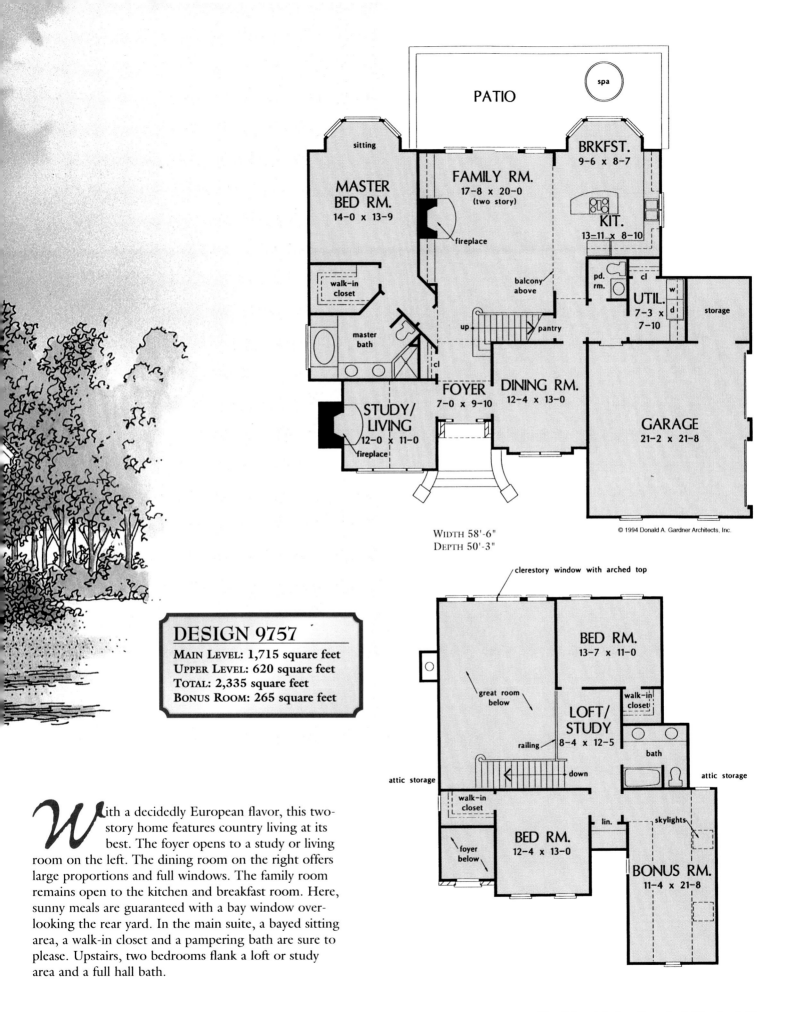

PATIO

spa

sitting

MASTER
BED RM.
14-0 x 13-9

FAMILY RM.
17-8 x 20-0
(two story)

BRKFST.
9-6 x 8-7

fireplace

KIT.
13-11 x 8-10

walk-in
closet

balcony
above

pd.
rm.

cl

UTIL.
7-3 x
7-10

w
d

storage

master
bath

up

pantry

cl

FOYER
7-0 x 9-10

DINING RM.
12-4 x 13-0

GARAGE
21-2 x 21-8

STUDY/
LIVING
12-0 x 11-0

fireplace

WIDTH 58'-6"
DEPTH 50'-3"

© 1994 Donald A. Gardner Architects, Inc.

clerestory window with arched top

great room
below

BED RM.
13-7 x 11-0

walk-in
closet

LOFT/
STUDY
8-4 x 12-5

bath

railing

down

attic storage

attic storage

walk-in
closet

lin.

skylights

foyer
below

BED RM.
12-4 x 13-0

BONUS RM.
11-4 x 21-8

DESIGN 9757

MAIN LEVEL: 1,715 square feet
UPPER LEVEL: 620 square feet
TOTAL: 2,335 square feet
BONUS ROOM: 265 square feet

With a decidedly European flavor, this two-story home features country living at its best. The foyer opens to a study or living room on the left. The dining room on the right offers large proportions and full windows. The family room remains open to the kitchen and breakfast room. Here, sunny meals are guaranteed with a bay window overlooking the rear yard. In the main suite, a bayed sitting area, a walk-in closet and a pampering bath are sure to please. Upstairs, two bedrooms flank a loft or study area and a full hall bath.

© 1994 Donald A. Gardner Architects, Inc.

B. NATHAN

THE *Paley*

Shuttered windows and a paneled front door create a warm welcome, while a sitting porch adds an aura of conviviality. Double pilasters and sidelights add formality to this brick elevation.

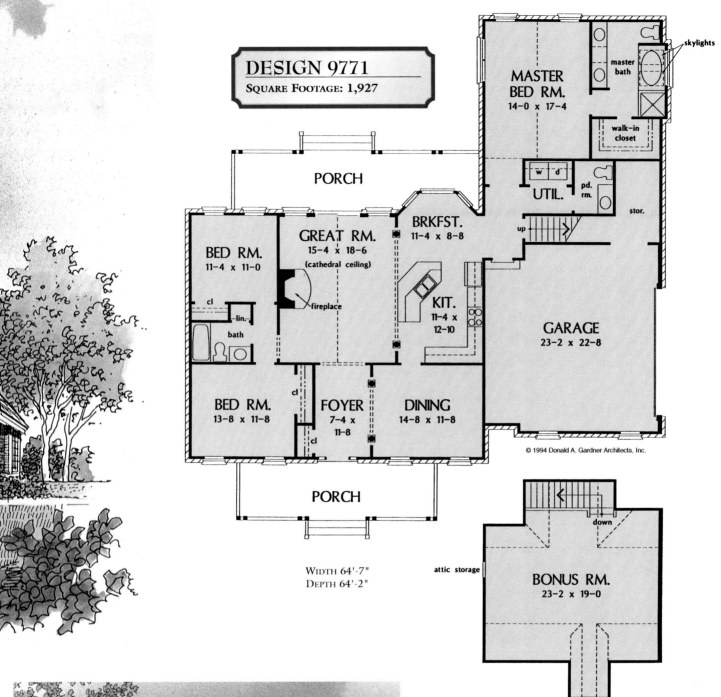

DESIGN 9771
SQUARE FOOTAGE: 1,927

PORCH

MASTER BED RM.
14-0 x 17-4

master bath

skylights

walk-in closet

UTIL.

w   d

pd. rm.

up

stor.

BRKFST.
11-4 x 8-8

GREAT RM.
15-4 x 18-6
(cathedral ceiling)

BED RM.
11-4 x 11-0

cl

lin.

bath

fireplace

KIT.
11-4 x 12-10

GARAGE
23-2 x 22-8

BED RM.
13-8 x 11-8

cl

FOYER
7-4 x 11-8

cl

DINING
14-8 x 11-8

© 1994 Donald A. Gardner Architects, Inc.

PORCH

WIDTH 64'-7"
DEPTH 64'-2"

attic storage

down

BONUS RM.
23-2 x 19-0

REAR VIEW

Sunlight takes center stage in this delightful country home. Each room has at least two windows to add warmth and radiance. Two bedrooms and a full bath are to the left of the foyer. To the right is the dining room, which leads into the L-shaped kitchen with a peninsular cooktop and connecting breakfast area with a bay window. The central great room offers a cathedral ceiling, a fireplace and access to the rear porch. The main suite is separated for privacy and features a lovely display of windows, a large walk-in closet and a luxurious whirlpool bath with skylights. Additional storage space is available in the garage and in the attic.

© 1994 Donald A. Gardner Architects, Inc.

B. NATHAN

THE *Woodsfield*

This plan offers the best of both worlds for those torn between traditional and country style. A quaint covered porch plays counterpoint to a traditional brick exterior, fusing casual and classic design.

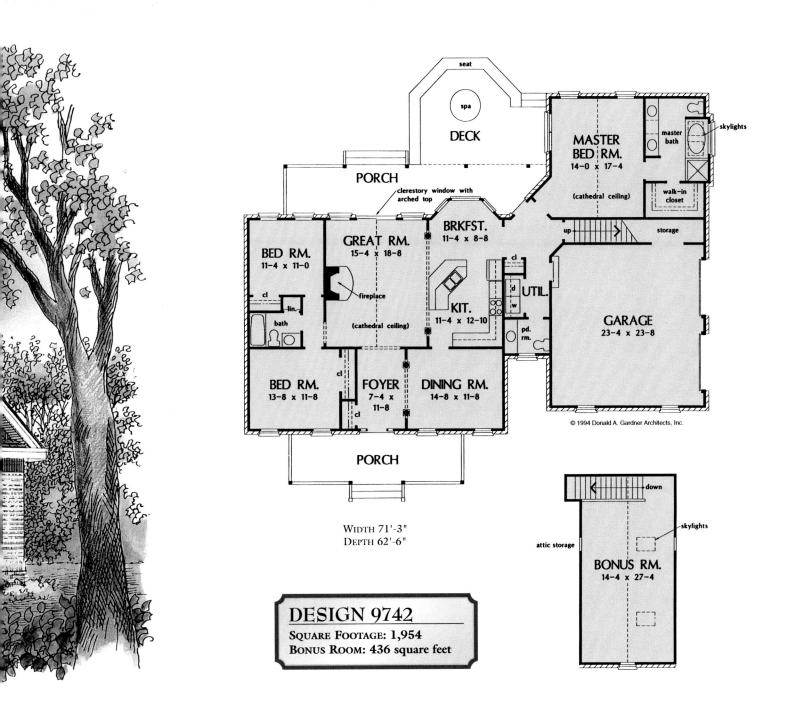

seat

spa

DECK

PORCH

clerestory window with arched top

MASTER BED RM.
14-0 x 17-4

(cathedral ceiling)

master bath

skylights

walk-in closet

up

storage

BRKFST.
11-4 x 8-8

GREAT RM.
15-4 x 18-8

BED RM.
11-4 x 11-0

cl

fireplace

(cathedral ceiling)

KIT.
11-4 x 12-10

cl

d
w

UTIL.

pd. rm.

GARAGE
23-4 x 23-8

lin.

bath

cl

BED RM.
13-8 x 11-8

FOYER
7-4 x 11-8

cl

DINING RM.
14-8 x 11-8

cl

© 1994 Donald A. Gardner Architects, Inc.

PORCH

WIDTH 71'-3"
DEPTH 62'-6"

down

skylights

attic storage

BONUS RM.
14-4 x 27-4

DESIGN 9742

SQUARE FOOTAGE: 1,954
BONUS ROOM: 436 square feet

REAR VIEW

*T*his beautiful brick country home offers style and comfort for an active family. Two covered porches and a rear deck with spa invite enjoyment of the outdoors, while a well-defined interior provides places to gather and entertain. A cathedral ceiling soars above the central great room, warmed by an extended-hearth fireplace and by sunlight through an arch-top clerestory window. A splendid main suite enjoys its own secluded wing, and offers a skylit whirlpool bath, a cathedral ceiling and private access to the deck. Two family bedrooms share a full bath on the opposite side of the plan.

THE *Graham*

*T*his stately, three-bedroom, one-story home exhibits sheer elegance with its large, arched windows, round columns, covered porch and brick veneer. In the foyer, natural light enters through arched windows in clerestory dormers. In the great room, a dramatic cathedral ceiling and a fireplace set the mood. Through gracious, round columns, the kitchen and breakfast room open up. For sleeping, turn to the main bedroom. Here, homeowners will enjoy a large, walk-in closet and a well-planned bath with a double-bowl vanity, a garden tub and a shower. Two additional bedrooms are located at the opposite end of the house for privacy.

WIDTH 60'-6"
DEPTH 50'-9"

DESIGN 9728
SQUARE FOOTAGE: 1,576

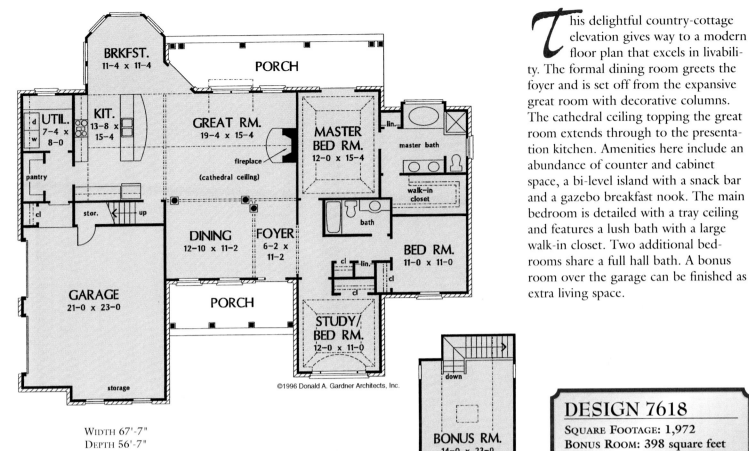

BRKFST.
11-4 x 11-4

PORCH

UTIL.
7-4 x
8-0

KIT.
13-8 x
15-4

GREAT RM.
19-4 x 15-4

MASTER
BED RM.
12-0 x 15-4

pantry

fireplace

(cathedral ceiling)

master bath

cl

stor.

up

walk-in
closet

bath

DINING
12-10 x 11-2

FOYER
6-2 x
11-2

GARAGE
21-0 x 23-0

PORCH

BED RM.
11-0 x 11-0

cl   lin.

cl

storage

STUDY/
BED RM.
12-0 x 11-0

©1996 Donald A. Gardner Architects, Inc.

WIDTH 67'-7"
DEPTH 56'-7"

down

BONUS RM.
14-0 x 23-0

skylights

DESIGN 7618
SQUARE FOOTAGE: 1,972
BONUS ROOM: 398 square feet

THE *Devon*

*T*his delightful country-cottage elevation gives way to a modern floor plan that excels in livability. The formal dining room greets the foyer and is set off from the expansive great room with decorative columns. The cathedral ceiling topping the great room extends through to the presentation kitchen. Amenities here include an abundance of counter and cabinet space, a bi-level island with a snack bar and a gazebo breakfast nook. The main bedroom is detailed with a tray ceiling and features a lush bath with a large walk-in closet. Two additional bedrooms share a full hall bath. A bonus room over the garage can be finished as extra living space.

© 1996 Donald A. Gardner Architects, Inc.

B. NATHAN.

Traditional designs for today's lifestyles **175**

© 1990 Donald A. Gardner Architects, Inc.

B. NATHAN

THE *Rothschild*

Elegant details abound in this French-influenced, one-story home with arched windows, round columns and a rich, brick veneer. A dramatic entry announces an interior full of amenities.

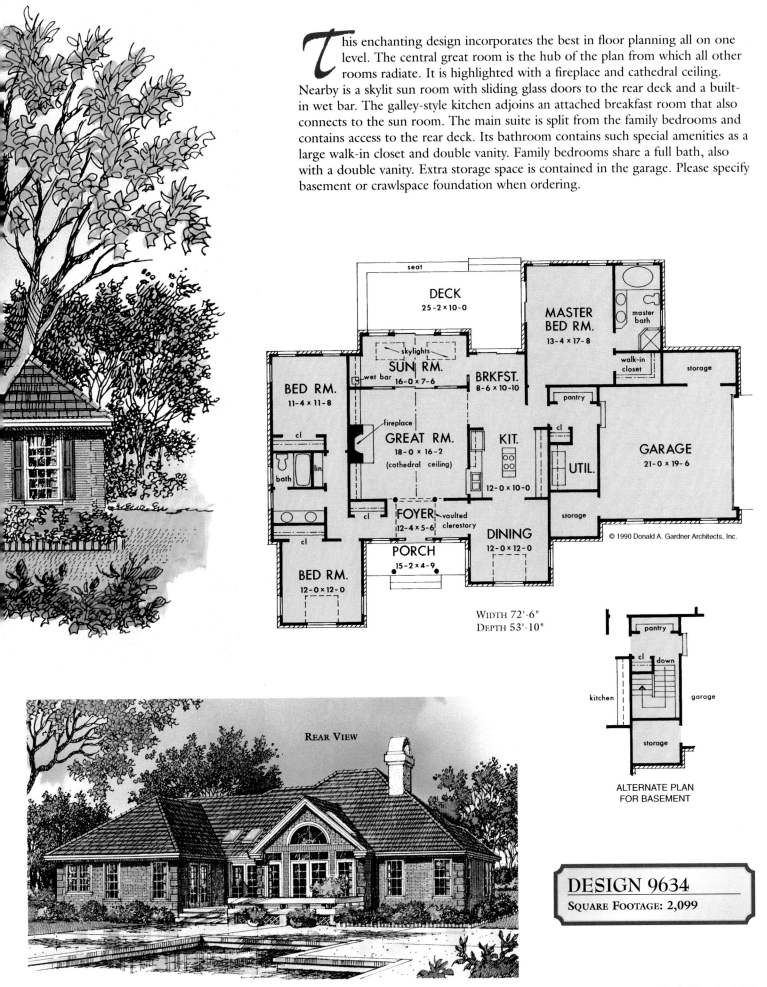

This enchanting design incorporates the best in floor planning all on one level. The central great room is the hub of the plan from which all other rooms radiate. It is highlighted with a fireplace and cathedral ceiling. Nearby is a skylit sun room with sliding glass doors to the rear deck and a built-in wet bar. The galley-style kitchen adjoins an attached breakfast room that also connects to the sun room. The main suite is split from the family bedrooms and contains access to the rear deck. Its bathroom contains such special amenities as a large walk-in closet and double vanity. Family bedrooms share a full bath, also with a double vanity. Extra storage space is contained in the garage. Please specify basement or crawlspace foundation when ordering.

DECK
25-2 × 10-0

MASTER
BED RM.
13-4 × 17-8

master bath

walk-in closet

storage

seat

skylights

SUN RM.
16-0 × 7-6

wet bar

BRKFST.
8-6 × 10-10

pantry

BED RM.
11-4 × 11-8

cl

bath

lin

fireplace

GREAT RM.
18-0 × 16-2
(cathedral ceiling)

KIT.
12-0 × 10-0

cl

UTIL.

GARAGE
21-0 × 19-6

cl

FOYER
12-4 × 5-6

vaulted clerestory

storage

DINING
12-0 × 12-0

© 1990 Donald A. Gardner Architects, Inc.

BED RM.
12-0 × 12-0

PORCH
15-2 × 4-9

WIDTH 72'-6"
DEPTH 53'-10"

pantry

cl down

kitchen

garage

storage

ALTERNATE PLAN
FOR BASEMENT

REAR VIEW

DESIGN 9634
SQUARE FOOTAGE: 2,099

THE *Herndon*

An artful combination of corner quoins and shuttered windows with sunburst accents decorate a distinctive European-style exterior. This traditional home combines great warmth with unmistakable elegance.

© 1993 Donald A. Gardner Architects, Inc.

This home features large arched windows, round columns, a covered porch and brick veneer siding. The arched window in the clerestory above the entrance provides natural light to the interior. The great room boasts a cathedral ceiling, a fireplace, built-in cabinets and bookshelves. Sliding glass doors lead to the sun room. The L-shaped kitchen services the dining room, the breakfast area, and the great room. The main suite, with a fireplace, uses a private passage to the deck and its spa. Three additional bedrooms—one could serve as a study—are at the other end of the house for privacy.

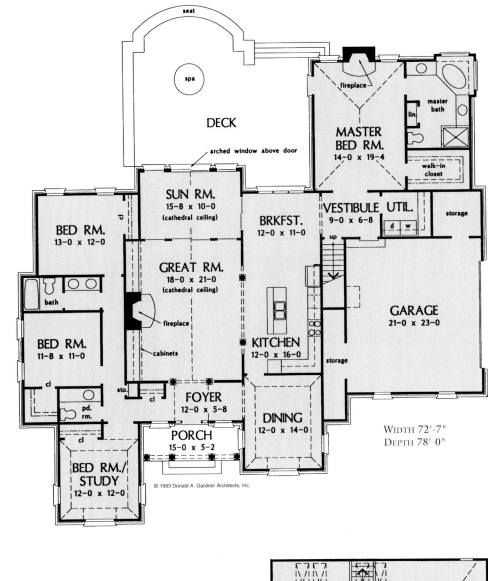

seat

spa

DECK

arched window above door

fireplace

master bath

MASTER BED RM.
14-0 x 19-4

lin

walk-in closet

SUN RM.
15-8 x 10-0
(cathedral ceiling)

BRKFST.
12-0 x 11-0

VESTIBULE UTIL.
9-0 x 6-8

storage

BED RM.
13-0 x 12-0

cl

GREAT RM.
18-0 x 21-0
(cathedral ceiling)

up

d   w

bath

fireplace

KITCHEN
12-0 x 16-0

GARAGE
21-0 x 23-0

BED RM.
11-8 x 11-0

cabinets

storage

cl

sto.

FOYER
12-0 x 5-8

cl

pd. rm.

DINING
12-0 x 14-0

WIDTH 72'-7"
DEPTH 78'-0"

cl

PORCH
15-0 x 5-2

© 1993 Donald A. Gardner Architects, Inc.

BED RM./ STUDY
12-0 x 12-0

DESIGN 9709
SQUARE FOOTAGE: 2,663
BONUS ROOM: 653 square feet

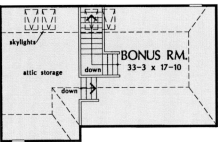

skylights

attic storage

BONUS RM.
33-3 x 17-10

down

down

© 1998 Donald A. Gardner, Inc.

THE *Vancouver*

Multi-pane windows complement a stately front porch,
supported by two sets of columns, on this impressive
brick home. A glass-paneled entry introduces an
interior that's as appropriate for planned
entertaining as it is for family living.

An exquisite brick exterior wraps this stately tradition-al home in luxury, while its hip and gable roof add stature and elegance. An impressive two-story ceiling with clerestory dormers amplifies the great room with a fireplace, built-ins and access to the back porch. An enviable center island kitchen is open to the great room and bayed breakfast area for optimum togetherness. Topped with a tray ceiling, the main suite enjoys back-porch access, dual walk-ins and a luxurious bath. Upstairs, a balcony overlooks the foyer and great room. Two upstairs bedrooms feature vaulted ceil-ings, while a third boasts a private bath. Another hall bath, ample linen space and a bonus room finish the second floor.

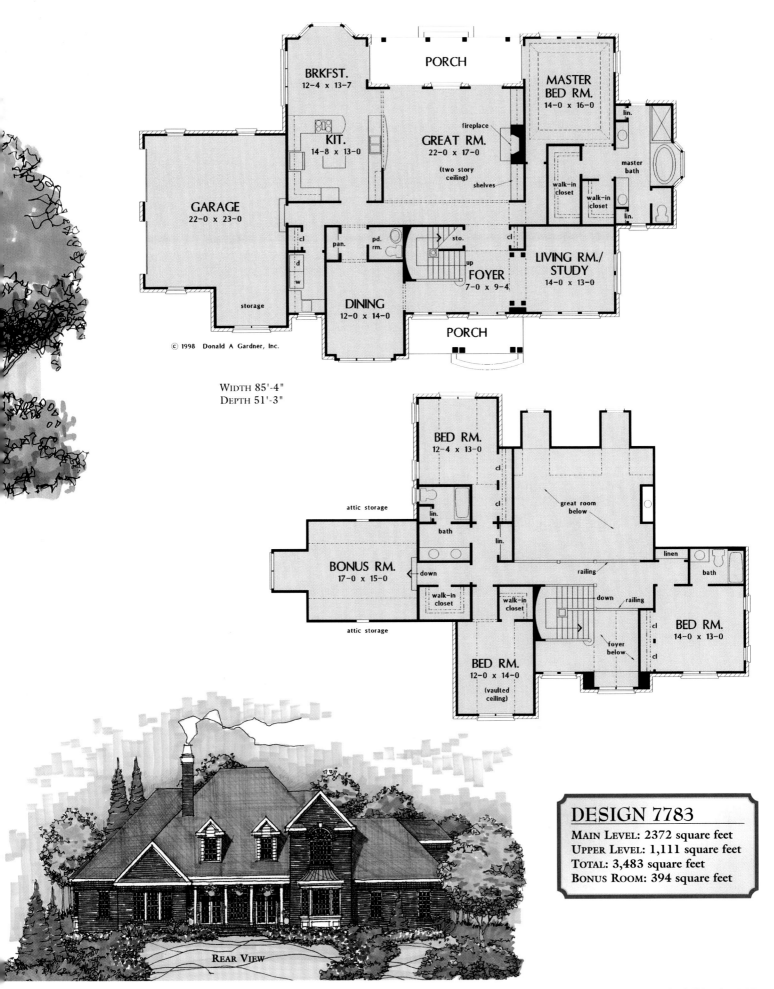

PORCH

BRKFST.
12-4 x 13-7

MASTER
BED RM.
14-0 x 16-0

KIT.
14-8 x 13-0

GREAT RM.
22-0 x 17-0

fireplace

lin.

GARAGE
22-0 x 23-0

(two story ceiling)

shelves

walk-in closet

master bath

walk-in closet

lin.

storage

cl

pan.

pd. rm.

sto.

up

cl

LIVING RM./
STUDY
14-0 x 13-0

d w

FOYER
7-0 x 9-4

DINING
12-0 x 14-0

PORCH

© 1998   Donald A Gardner, Inc.

WIDTH 85'-4"
DEPTH 51'-3"

BED RM.
12-4 x 13-0

attic storage

cl

great room
below

lin.

bath

BONUS RM.
17-0 x 15-0

cl

lin.

linen

bath

down

railing

attic storage

walk-in closet

walk-in closet

down

railing

BED RM.
14-0 x 13-0

cl

BED RM.
12-0 x 14-0

(vaulted ceiling)

foyer
below

cl

REAR VIEW

DESIGN 7783

MAIN LEVEL: 2372 square feet
UPPER LEVEL: 1,111 square feet
TOTAL: 3,483 square feet
BONUS ROOM: 394 square feet

Traditional designs for today's lifestyles **181**

© 1996 Donald A. Gardner Architects, Inc.

THE *Rousseau*

Asymmetrical gables and a keystone arch lend a gentle
European flavor to this stunning stucco and brick home.
A dramatic entry is enhanced by a paneled door with
an exquisite multi-pane fanlight and sidelights.

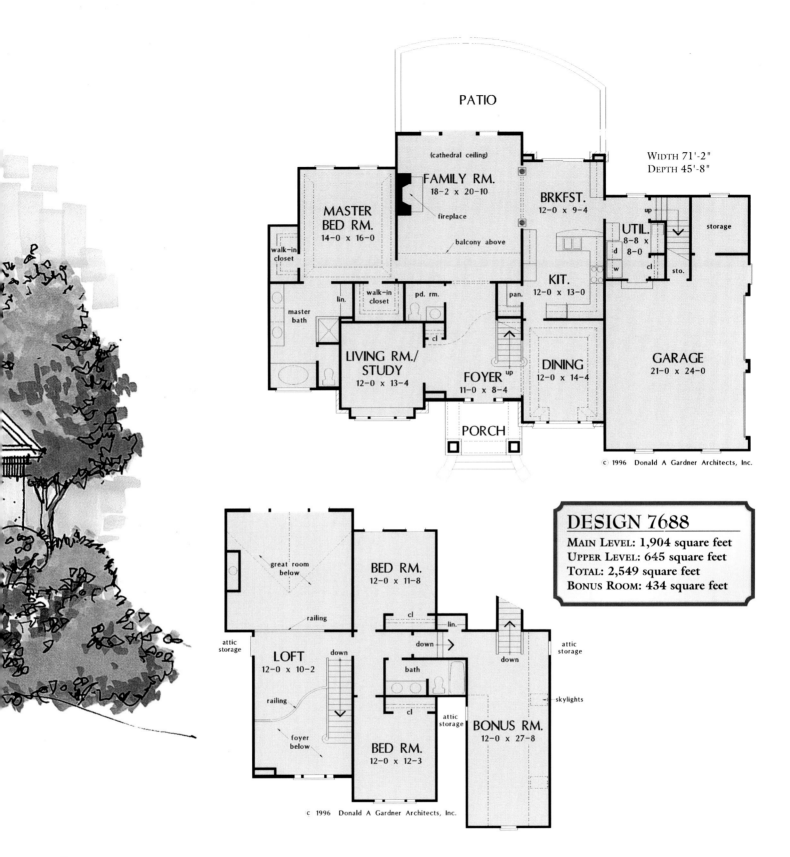

PATIO

(cathedral ceiling)

FAMILY RM.
18-2 x 20-10

fireplace

BRKFST.
12-0 x 9-4

WIDTH 71'-2"
DEPTH 45'-8"

MASTER
BED RM.
14-0 x 16-0

balcony above

up

storage

UTIL.
8-8 x
8-0

walk-in
closet

d

KIT.
12-0 x 13-0

w

cl

sto.

master
bath

lin.

walk-in
closet

pd. rm.

pan.

GARAGE
21-0 x 24-0

cl

LIVING RM./
STUDY
12-0 x 13-4

FOYER
11-0 x 8-4

up

DINING
12-0 x 14-4

PORCH

(c) 1996 Donald A Gardner Architects, Inc.

great room
below

railing

BED RM.
12-0 x 11-8

attic
storage

LOFT
12-0 x 10-2

down

cl

lin.

down

up

attic
storage

bath

down

skylights

railing

down

foyer
below

cl

attic
storage

BONUS RM.
12-0 x 27-8

BED RM.
12-0 x 12-3

c 1996   Donald A Gardner Architects, Inc.

DESIGN 7688

MAIN LEVEL: 1,904 square feet
UPPER LEVEL: 645 square feet
TOTAL: 2,549 square feet
BONUS ROOM: 434 square feet

*T*his stucco home contrasts gently curved arches with gables, and uses large multi-pane windows to flood the interior with natural light. Square pillars form an impressive entry, leading to a two-story foyer. The living room is set apart from the informal area of the house, and could serve as a cozy study instead. The U-shaped kitchen is centrally located between the dining room and a sunny breakfast nook.

Nearby, a utility room leads to back stairs and a two-car garage. The back patio can be reached from both the breakfast nook and the family room, which features a cathedral ceiling and a fireplace. The main suite on the first floor offers two walk-in closets and a bath with twin vanities, a garden tub and a separate shower. In addition to two family bedrooms and a bath, the second floor contains a loft and a bonus room.

© 1998 Donald A. Gardner, Inc.

culhen

THE *Sable Ridge*

Designed for sloping lots, this superb stone and stucco home takes advantage of rear views, making it a great lakeside or mountain retreat. To the front, a sunny breakfast room opens to a covered porch that extends to the garage for the family's convenience.

A stone-and-stucco exterior and exquisite window detailing give this home its Mediterranean appeal. A covered porch connects the garage to the main house via the breakfast room. The main suite includes two walk-in closets and a bath with separate vanities. Two family bedrooms in the basement feature walk-in closets and share a compartmented bath and a media/recreation room. Both bedrooms have private access to the patio. A utility room and storage room complete the basement level. This home is designed with a walk-out basement.

Main Level

PORCH

DINING
12-0 x 12-2

MASTER BED RM.
15-0 x 13-4
(cathedral ceiling)

fireplace

GREAT RM.
20-0 x 16-4
(cathedral ceiling)

KITCHEN
17-4 x 11-4

walk-in closet

walk-in closet

railing

down

pan.

BRKFST.
11-2 x 9-2

lin.

FOYER
6-8 x cl
7-4

pd. rm.

master bath

PORCH

PORCH

WIDTH 54'-0"
DEPTH 40'-8"

© 1998 Donald A Gardner, Inc.

covered walkway

GARAGE
23-0 x 23-0

Lower Level

PATIO

COVERED PATIO

bath

lin.

BED RM.
11-6 x 13-0

walk-in closet

walk-in closet

BED RM.
12-0 x 13-0

MEDIA/ REC. RM.
16-6 x 31-10

STORAGE
(unfinished)

UTIL.
8-10 x 6-10

d   w

up

REAR VIEW

DESIGN 7665

MAIN LEVEL: 1,472 square feet
LOWER LEVEL: 1,211 square feet
TOTAL: 2,683 square feet

THE *Legacy*

Round columns, gentle arches and twin dormers
highlight the exterior of this country classic.
The sunburst window accent in the center
gable is subtly repeated on both wings of the
house, to unite the architectural theme.

A stunning combination of both country and traditional exterior elements creates a timeless facade for this exquisite estate home. A dramatic two-story rotunda makes a great first impression, followed by equally impressive dual staircases and a large great room with a cathedral ceiling and overlooking curved balcony and loft. The spacious kitchen easily serves the dining room, breakfast area and great room. Note the walk-in pantry. The media/recreation room features a wall of built-in cabinets to house television and stereo equipment. More oasis than bedroom, the main suite is amplified by a deep tray ceiling and enjoys a fireplace, built-in dressing cabinetry, two walk-in closets and a luxurious bath with every amenity. Two bedrooms, two baths and an oversized bonus room are on the second floor.

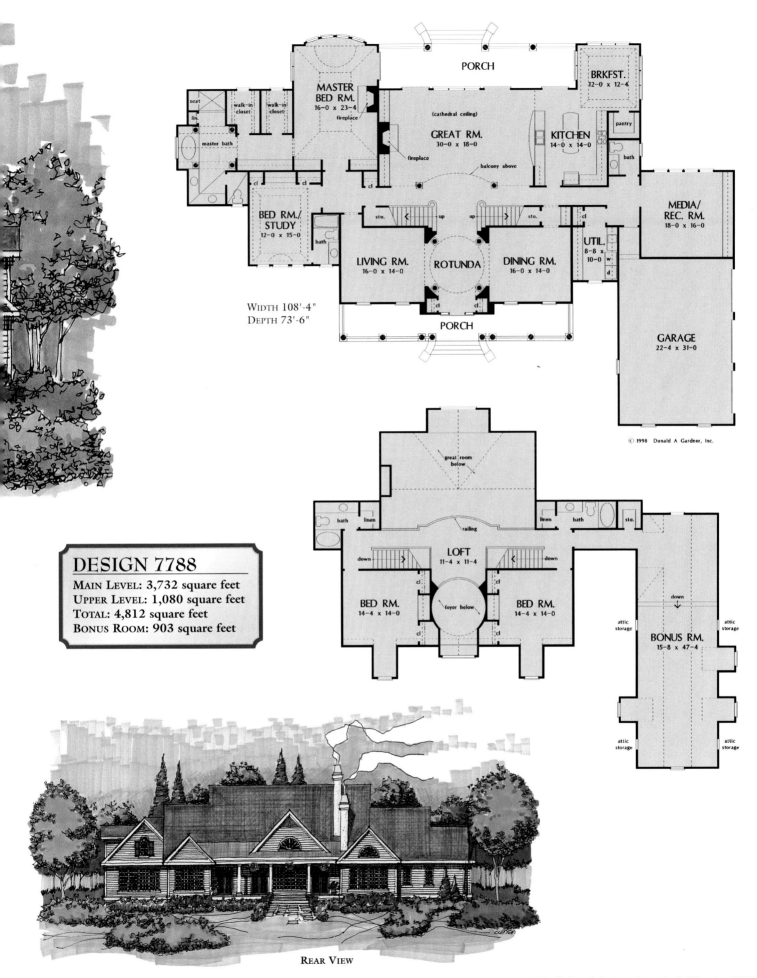

PORCH

MASTER
BED RM.
16-0 x 23-4

fireplace

seat

lin.

walk-in
closet

walk-in
closet

master bath

(cathedral ceiling)

GREAT RM.
30-0 x 18-0

fireplace

balcony above

BRKFST.
12-0 x 12-4

KITCHEN
14-0 x 14-0

pantry

bath

cl

cl

cl

BED RM./
STUDY
12-0 x 15-0

bath

sto.

up

up

sto.

cl

UTIL.
8-8 x
10-0

w

d

MEDIA/
REC. RM.
18-0 x 16-0

LIVING RM.
16-0 x 14-0

ROTUNDA

DINING RM.
16-0 x 14-0

WIDTH 108'-4"
DEPTH 73'-6"

cl

cl

PORCH

GARAGE
22-4 x 31-0

© 1998 Donald A Gardner, Inc.

great room
below

bath

linen

linen

bath

sto.

railing

down

LOFT
11-4 x 11-4

down

DESIGN 7788

MAIN LEVEL: 3,732 square feet
UPPER LEVEL: 1,080 square feet
TOTAL: 4,812 square feet
BONUS ROOM: 903 square feet

BED RM.
14-4 x 14-0

cl

foyer below

cl

BED RM.
14-4 x 14-0

cl

cl

down

attic
storage

attic
storage

BONUS RM.
15-8 x 47-4

attic
storage

attic
storage

REAR VIEW

Important Extras To Do The Job Right!

Introducing eight important planning and construction aids developed by our professionals to help you succeed in your home-building project.

Materials Lists

For many of the designs in our portfolio, we offer a customized materials take-off that is invaluable in planning and estimating the cost of your new home. This Materials List outlines the quantity, type and size of materials needed to build your house (with the exception of mechanical system items). Included are framing lumber, windows and doors, kitchen and bath cabinetry, rough and finish hardware, and much more. This handy list helps you or your builder cost out materials and serves as a reference sheet when you're compiling bids.A Materials List cannot be ordered before blueprints are ordered.

(Note: Because of the diversity of local building codes, our Materials List does not include mechanical materials.)

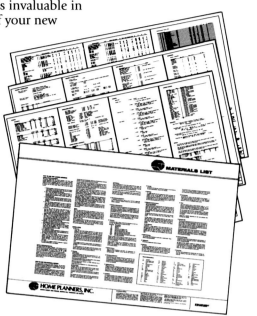

Quote One®
Summary Cost Report/Materials Cost Report

A new service for estimating the cost of building select designs, the Quote One® system is available in two separate stages: The Summary Cost Report and the Materials Cost Report.

The Summary Cost Report is the first stage in the package and shows the total cost per square foot for your chosen home in your zip-code area and then breaks that cost down into various categories showing the costs for building materials, labor and installation. The total cost for the report (which includes three grades: Budget, Standard and Custom) is just $29.95 for one home, and additionals are only $14.95. These reports allow you to evaluate your building budget and compare the costs of building a variety of homes in your area.

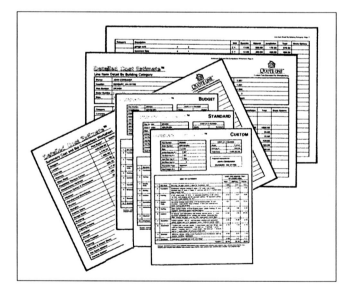

Make even more informed decisions about your home-building project with the second phase of our package, our Materials Cost Report. This tool is invaluable in planning and estimating the cost of your new home. The material and installation (labor and equipment) cost is shown for each of over 1,000 line items provided in the Materials List (Standard grade), which is included when you purchase this estimating tool. It allows you to determine building costs for your specific zip-code area and for your chosen home design. Space is allowed for additional estimates from contractors and subcontractors, such as for mechanical materials, which are not included in our packages. This invaluable tool is available for a price of $120 ($130 for a schedule C4–L1 plan), which includes a Materials List. A Materials Cost Report cannot be ordered before blueprints are ordered.

The Quote One® program is continually updated with new plans. If you are interested in a plan that is not indicated as Quote One®, please call to verify the status. To order these invaluable reports, use the order form on page 191 or call **1-800-521-6797**.

DETAIL SETS

Each set is an excellent tool that will add to your understanding of these technical subjects and deal more confidently with subcontractors.

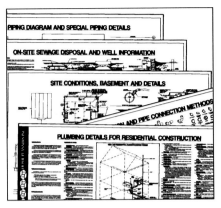

PLUMBING

If you want to know more about the complete plumbing system, these 24x36-inch detail sheets will prove very useful. Prepared to meet requirements of the National Plumbing Code, these six fact-filled sheets give general information on pipe schedules, fittings, sump-pump details, water-softener hookups, septic system details and much more. Color-coded sheets include a glossary of terms.

ELECTRICAL

Prepared to meet requirements of the National Electrical Code, these comprehensive 24x36-inch drawings come packed with helpful information, including wire sizing, switch-installation schematics, cable-routing details, appliance wattage, doorbell hookups, typical service panel circuitry and much more. Six sheets are bound together and color-coded for easy reference. A glossary of terms is also included.

11"x17" COLOR RENDERING

Full-color renderings suitable for framing are available for all of the plans contained in this book. For prices and additional information, please see page 190 or call the toll-free number listed below.

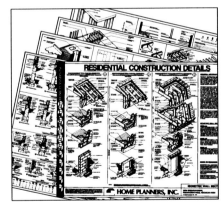

CONSTRUCTION

To help you understand how your house will be built—and offer additional techniques—this set of drawings depicts the materials and methods used to build foundations, fireplaces, walls, floors and roofs. Where appropriate, the drawings show acceptable alternatives. These six sheets will answer questions for the advanced do-it-yourselfer or home planner.

MECHANICAL

This package will help you make informed decisions and communicate with subcontractors about heating and cooling systems. The 24x36-inch drawings contain instructions and samples that allow you to make simple load calculations and preliminary sizing and costing analysis. Covered are today's most commonly used systems from heat pumps to solar fuel systems. The package is full of illustrations and diagrams to help you visualize components and how they relate to one another.

SPECIFICATION OUTLINE

This 16-page document is critical to building your house correctly. Designed to be filled in by you or your builder, this book lists 166 stages or items crucial to the building process. It provides a comprehensive review of the construction process and helps in choosing materials. When combined with the blueprints, a signed contract, and a schedule, it becomes a legal document and record for the building of your home.

To Order, Call Toll Free
1-800-521-6797

To add these important extras to your Blueprint Package, simply indicate your choices on the order form on page 191 or call us toll free 1-800-521-6797.

To use the index below, refer to the design number listed in numerical order (a page reference is also given). Note the price index letter and refer to the House Blueprint Price Schedule on this page for the cost of one, four, or eight sets of blueprints or the cost of a reproducible set. Additional prices are shown for identical and reverse blueprint sets. All plans have Materials Lists.

Some plans are also part of our Quote One® estimating service and are indicated by this symbol:🏠.

To Order: Fill in and send the order form on page 191, or if you prefer, fax to 1-800-224-6699 or 520-544-3086—or call toll free 1-800-521-6797 or 1-800-297-8200.

Blueprint Price Schedule
(Prices guaranteed through December 31, 2000)

Tiers	1-set Study Package	4-set Building Package	8-set Building Package	1-set Reproducible Vellums
A2	$440	$480	$540	$660
A3	$480	$520	$580	$720
A4	$520	$560	$620	$780
C1	$560	$600	$660	$840
C2	$600	$640	$700	$900
C3	$650	$690	$750	$950
C4	$700	$740	$800	$1000
L1	$750	$790	$850	$1050

Options for plans in Tiers A2–L1

Additional Identical Blueprints in same order for "A2–L1" price plans	$50 per set
Reverse Blueprints (mirror image) with 4- or 8-set order for "A2–L1" price plans	$50 fee per order
Full Reverse Blueprints (right reading) with 4- or 8-set order for "A2–L1" price plans	$150 fee per order
Specification Outlines	$10 each
Materials Lists for "A2–C3" price plans	$60 each
Materials Lists for "C4–L1" price plans	$70 each
11"x17" Color Rendering, Front Perspective	$70 each

IMPORTANT NOTES
The 1-set study package is marked "not for construction."
Prices for 4- or 8-set Building Packages honored only at time of original order.

BEFORE YOU ORDER . . .

Before filling out the coupon at right or calling us on our Toll-Free Blueprint Hotline, you may want to learn more about our services and products. Here's some information you will find helpful.

Quick Turnaround
We process every blueprint order from our office within two business days. Because of this quick turnaround, we won't send a formal notice acknowledging receipt of your order.

Our Exchange Policy
Since blueprints are printed in response to your order, we cannot honor requests for refunds. However, we will exchange your entire first order for an equal number of blueprints at a price of $50 for the first set and $10 for each additional set; $70 total exchange fee for 4 sets; $100 total exchange fee for 8 sets . . . *plus* the difference in cost if exchanging for a design in a higher price bracket or *less* the difference in cost if exchanging for a design in a lower price bracket. One exchange is allowed within a year of purchase date. (Vellums are not exchangeable.) All sets from the first order must be returned before the exchange can take place. Please add $18 for postage and handling via Regular Service; $30 via Priority Service; $40 via Express Service. Returns and cancellations are subject to a 20% restocking fee, and shipping and handling charges are not refundable.

About Reverse Blueprints
If you want to build in reverse of the plan as shown, we will include any number of reverse blueprints (mirror image) from a 4- or 8-set package for an additional fee of $50. Although lettering and dimensions will appear backward, reverses will be a useful aid if you decide to flop the plan.

Architectural and Engineering Seals
Some cities and states are now requiring that a licensed architect or engineer review and "seal" a blueprint, or officially approve it, prior to construction due to concerns over energy costs, safety and other factors. Prior to application for a building permit or the start of actual construction, we strongly advise that you consult your local building official who can tell you if such a review is required.

Local Building Codes and Zoning Requirements
At the time of creation, our plans are drawn to specifications published by the Building Officials and Code Administrators (BOCA) International, Inc.; the Southern Building Code Congress (SBCCI) International, Inc.; the International Conference of Building Officials; or the Council of American Building Officials (CABO). Our plans are designed to meet or exceed national building standards. Because of the great differences in geography and climate throughout the United States and Canada, each state, county and municipality has its own building codes, zone requirements, ordinances and building regulations. Your plan may need to be modified to comply with local requirements regarding snow loads, energy codes, soil and seismic conditions and a wide range of other matters. In addition, you may need to obtain permits or inspections from local governments before and in the course of construction. Prior to using blueprints ordered from us, we strongly advise that you consult a licensed architect or engineer—and speak with your local building official—before applying for any permit or beginning construction. We authorize the use of our blueprints on the express condition that you strictly comply with all local building codes, zoning requirements and other applicable laws, regulations, ordinances and requirements.

Notice: Plans for homes to be built in Nevada must be re-drawn by a Nevada-registered professional. Consult your building official for more information on this subject.

Foundation and Exterior Wall Changes
Most of our plans are drawn with either a full or partial basement foundation. Depending on your specific climate or regional building practices, you may wish to change this basement to a slab or crawlspace. Most professional contractors and builders can easily adapt your plans to alternate foundation types. Likewise, most can easily change 2x4 wall construction to 2x6, or vice versa.

Disclaimer
We and the designers we work with have put substantial care and effort into the creation of our blueprints. However, because we cannot provide on-site consultation, supervision and control over actual construction, and because of the great variance in local building requirements, building practices and soil, seismic, weather and other conditions, WE CANNOT MAKE ANY WARRANTY, EXPRESS OR IMPLIED, WITH RESPECT TO THE CONTENT OR USE OF OUR BLUEPRINTS, INCLUDING BUT NOT LIMITED TO ANY WARRANTY OF MERCHANTABILITY OR OF FITNESS FOR A PARTICULAR PURPOSE.

Terms and Conditions
These designs are protected under the terms of United States Copyright Law and may not be copied or reproduced in any way, by any means, unless you have purchased Sepias or Reproducibles which clearly indicate your right to copy or reproduce. We authorize the use of your chosen design as an aid in the construction of one single-family home only. You may not use this design to build a second or multiple dwellings without purchasing another blueprint or blueprints or paying additional design fees.

BLUEPRINTS ARE NOT REFUNDABLE EXCHANGES ONLY

ORDER FORM

HOME PLANNERS, LLC, wholly owned by Hanley-Wood, Inc.
3275 WEST INA ROAD, SUITE 110
TUCSON, AZ 85741

THE BASIC BLUEPRINT PACKAGE
Rush me the following (please refer to the Price Schedule & Plans Index on page 190):

_____ Set(s) of blueprints for plan number(s) _____ $_____
_____ Set(s) of vellums for plan number(s) _____ $_____
_____ Additional identical blueprints (standard or reverse)
          in same order @ $50 per set. $_____
_____ Reverse blueprint fee @ $50 per order. $_____
_____ Full Reverse blueprint fee @ $150 per order. $_____
_____ 11"x17" Color Rendering for plan number(s) _____ $_____
_____ Specification Outlines @ $10 each. $_____
_____ Materials List for A2–C3 price plans @ $60 each. $_____
_____ Add $10 for a schedule C4–L1 plan.
_____ Detail Sets @ $14.95 each; any two for $22.95;
          any three for $29.95; all four for $39.95 (Save $19.85). $_____
          ❏ Plumbing ❏ Electrical ❏ Construction ❏ Mechanical
          (These helpful details provide general constuction
          advice and are not specific to any single plan.)
_____ Quote One® Summary Cost Report @ $29.95 for 1,
          $14.95 for each additional, for plans _____ $_____
          Building location: City _____ Zip Code _____
_____ Quote One® Materials Cost Report @ $120 or $130
          for plans _____ $_____
          (Must be purchased with Blueprints set; Materials List included)
          Building location: City _____ Zip Code _____

POSTAGE AND HANDLING	1–3 sets	4 or more sets
CARRIER DELIVERY Signature is required for all deliveries. No CODS (requires street address—No P.O. Boxes)		
•Regular Service (Allow 7–10 business days delivery)	❏ $15.00	❏ $18.00
•Priority (Allow 4–5 business days delivery)	❏ $20.00	❏ $30.00
•Express (Allow 3 business days delivery)	❏ $30.00	❏ $40.00
CERTIFIED MAIL (requires signature) Use if no street address available. Allow 7–10 days delivery.	❏ $20.00	❏ $30.00
Note: All delivery times are from date Blueprint Package is shipped.	**OVERSEAS AIR MAIL DELIVERY** Phone, Fax or Mail for quote	

POSTAGE (From box above) $_____
SUBTOTAL $_____
SALES TAX (AZ, MI, & WA residents, please add appropriate
          state and local sales taxes.) $_____

TOTAL (Subtotal and tax) $_____

YOUR ADDRESS (please print)
Name_____
Street_____
City _____State _____ZIP _____
Daytime telephone number (_____)_____

FOR CREDIT CARD ORDERS ONLY
Please fill in the information below:

Credit card number _____
Exp. Date: Month/Year _____
Check one ❏ Visa ❏ MasterCard ❏ Discover Card ❏ American Express

Signature _____
Please check appropriate box:
          ❏ Licensed Builder-Contractor
          ❏ Homeowner

TO ORDER: 1-800-521-6797 or 520-297-8200 Order Form Key
OR FAX: 1-800-224-6699 or 520-544-3086 TB70
For customer service, call toll free 1-888-690-1116.

THE BLUEPRINT PACKAGE

Each set of home plan blueprints is a related gathering of plans, diagrams, measurements, details and specifications that precisely show how your new residence will come together. Each home design receives careful attention and planning from the expert staff of Donald A. Gardner Architects, Inc. to ensure quality and buildability.

Here's what the package includes:

- ❖ Designer's rendering of front elevation
- ❖ Foundation and dimensioned floor plans
- ❖ Building cross-sections
- ❖ Selected interior elevations
- ❖ Fireplace and cabinet elevations
- ❖ Floor and roof framing plans
- ❖ Electrical plans
- ❖ All exterior elevations
- ❖ Door and window sizes
- ❖ Roof plan and exterior details

Reversed plans are mirror-image sets with lettering and dimensioning shown backwards. To receive plans in reverse, specifically request this when placing your order. Since lettering and dimensions appear backward on reverse blueprints, we suggest you order one set reversed for siting and the rest as shown for construction purposes. Full reverse blueprints (right reading) are also available. (See page 190 for additional information.)

Plans are designed to meet the requirements of the *Council of American Building Officials (CABO) One and Two Family Dwelling Code*. Because codes are subject to various changes and interpretations, the purchaser is responsible for compliance with all local building codes, ordinances, site conditions, subdivision restrictions and structural elements by having their builder review the plans to ensure compliance. We also recommend that you have an engineer in your area review your plans before actual construction begins.

☎ ORDER TOLL FREE 1-800-521-6797
After you've looked over The Blueprint Package and additional products on pages 188-189, simply mail the order form on page 191 or call toll free on our Blueprint Hotline: **1-800-521-6797**. We're ready and eager to serve you.